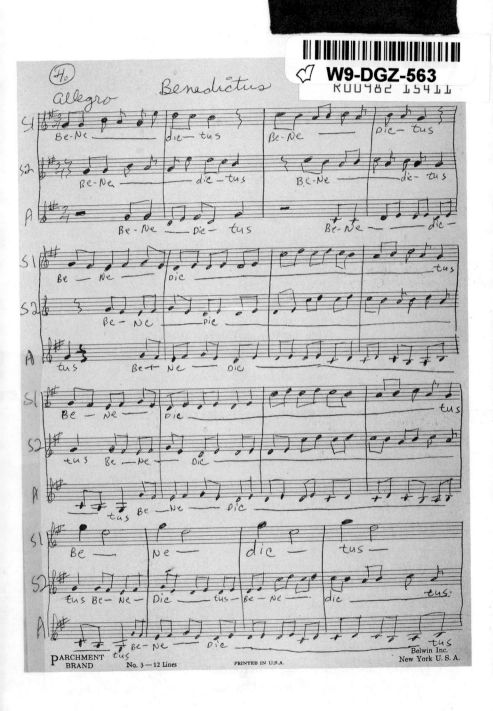

Benedictus

Allegro

PARCHMENT BRAND   No. 3—12 Lines   PRINTED IN U.S.A.   Belwin Inc. New York U.S.A.

Also by Rinna Evelyn Wolfe

Mary McLeod Bethune, 1992
Charles Richard Drew, M.D., 1991
The Singing Pope, 1980

End papers: Calvin wrote Benedictus *at age 15.*
He stopped composing when he felt he was creating "very bad Mozart."

THE CALVIN SIMMONS STORY
OR
"DON'T CALL ME MAESTRO"

California children meet their first conductor at the Oakland Museum.

The Calvin Simmons Story
Or
"Don't Call Me Maestro!"

by Rinna Evelyn Wolfe

Muse Wood Press • Berkeley, California

Muse Wood Press
256 Fairlawn Drive
Berkeley, California 94708
(510) 845-0507

© 1994 by Rinna Evelyn Wolfe

Book and Cover Design: Augustus F. Ginnochio
Cover Photograph: Robert Reiter©

Photographs courtesy of Madi Bacon, Cathe Centorbe, Guy Gravett, Ken Howard, Carolyn Mason Jones, Mary Lawrence, Louise McTernan, Richard Meyer, Betty Jane Nevis, © Ira Nowinski, Robert Reiter, Henry Calvin Simmons, Sedge Thomson, Jim Widess and the British Tourist Authority, Glyndebourne Festival Opera, the Paramount Theater, San Diego Opera and the San Francisco Opera.

Library of Congress Catalog Card Number 94-076622

Wolfe, Rinna © 1994

The Calvin Simmons Story or "Don't Call Me Maestro"
by Rinna Evelyn Wolfe includes index and photos:
Summary: A biogaphy of the first African American conductor of a
            a major United States Orchestra.

ISBN 0-9641449-0-5

1) Simmons, Calvin Eugene 1950 - 1982 - adult literature and biography 2) African American conductors - biography - adult and young adult literature 3) Teachers - United States history - music - opera, symphony.

First Edition 6 5 4 3 2 1

*In loving memory
of my mother, Pauline,
and my nephew, Marty*

*"Only they remain and
will endure, who touch
the sensitive hearts
of man."*
— Le Courbusier

Acknowledgements

I wish to thank Anne Fox, Frances Whitney, Marjorie Jackson, Jim Widess, Mary Rich and Kori Lockhart and especially Fred Tulan who over the years offered invaluable suggestions and editing advice. Their efforts on my behalf helped shape Calvin's biography.

Then, there are the many story-tellers. Without the sharing of their memories this book could never have been written.

Contributors were:

Donald Aird
Joseph Alessi
William Duncan Allen
Ernst Bacon
Madi Bacon
Martin Bernheimer
Marilyn Blanc
Richard Bradshaw
Sarah Chambers
Barbara Chevelier
Sir George Christie
Gale Cunningham
Tim Ericson
Robert Fahrner
Peggy Fahrner
Mathew Farruggio
Mars Fletcher
Richard Gaddes
Ross Gershenson
Tom Godfrey
Ruth Golden
Tom Brown-Gomez
Carol Handlemann
Nikki Li Hartliep
Edy Haysaki
Sasha Hourwich
Stanley Ibler
Judie Janowski
William Corbett Jones
Monroe Kanouse
Philip Kelsey

Jacqueline Benson-Kinley
Ed Korn
Eugene Kushner
Harold Lawrence
Sylvia Oden Lee
Heidi Lesemann
Marion Lever
Gary Levy
Kori Lockhart
Ethel London
Mary Maehl
Larry Maisel
Sharon Manuel
James Matheson
Carmen McRae
Louise McTernan
Marilyn Mercur
Zubin Mehta
Zaven Melikian
Dick Meyer
Janice Mickens
Kent Nagano
Carol Negro
Verez Olshausen
Rufus Olivier
Pat Olson
Peter Orth
David Reed
Julio Reyes
Halina Rodzinski
Evelyn de la Rosa

Max Rudolf
Gerhard Samuel
Ann Seamster
Irene Serkin
Etta Shapiro
Irwin Shapiro
Richard Shead
Charles Shere
Armenda Sneed
Henry Calvin Simmons
Mattie Pearl Simmons
Stephen Cobett Steinberg
Abina Sullivan
Doris Taboloff
Ruth Tapples
Sedge Thomson
Heuwell Tricuit
Paul Tobias
Marilyn Tucker
Fred Tulan
Bill Tull
Letha Turner
Morrie Turner
Dan Turpin
Ivan Van Peere
William Wahman
Gordon Waldear
Sidney Walker
Allan Yamamoto
Harold Youngsberg

And Diana Alvarez, La Shenda Hanzy, Soledad Padilla, Rhonda Riley, Lorraine Sloss and Kreisha Wright at the Calvin Simmons Junior High School.
To those whose names inadvertently may have been omitted, I ask your forgiveness.

I also appreciate the support given to this project by PALM (San Francisco Performing Arts Library Museum).

Contents

Contents

THE CALVIN SIMMONS STORY
or
DON'T CALL ME MAESTRO
by
Rinna Evelyn Wolfe

Beanpole thin, rail thin, Calvin usually stood a head taller than most boys his age. High-spirited, pulsating with unbounded energy, his body and legs rarely were still. His face seemed mostly large, soft brown eyes; his grin was contagious. Whenever Calvin smiled, everyone around him smiled too.

To close friends he was "Cal." In junior high school a gym teacher dubbed him Watusi after the African tribe of tall, thin warriors. It hurt at the time, but Calvin later said, "Eventually I got over that." Exaggerating, he added, "At thirteen I was seven feet tall! Disgusting!"

A school coach asked him to play basketball or go out for track and become a sprinter. Calvin did do high jumps for two or three months. He even joined the track team, but for just one week. "No sports for me," he told himself. "I'll go to gym but I'm not going to hurt my hands."

No, sports would not lead Calvin to fame and fortune. At an early age he trained his long, bony fingers to make music which ultimately would reach into the hearts of millions of people.

Calvin, age 26 months, stands proudly atop the family piano bench.

- I -
The Young Music Lover

When nine-year-old Calvin Simmons entered the San Francisco Calvary Presbyterian Church with his mother on a crisp September afternoon in 1959, his life opened to a new world. Inside mother and son separated. Mrs. Mattie Pearl Simmons joined other parents for doughnuts and coffee. Calvin blended in with about two dozen boys, waiting nervously for the San Francisco Boys Chorus annual tryouts.

One of his friends was already a member, so knowing what to expect, Calvin had come well prepared. The Chorus twice-a-week rehearsals, concerts and singing on the huge stage of the War Memorial Opera House appealed to him.

"Ready? C Major!" Calvin heard as the door to a nearby smaller room opened and a foursome of boys was ushered in. When Calvin's group moved inside, he watched from the sidelines, his eyes riveted on Madi Bacon, the Chorus Director. After a brief conversation, playing at the piano, Miss Bacon waved her hand for a boy to begin.

"Vuvah, vuvah, vuvah, vuvah," the boy sang, his voice running up and down the scale.

"Good, now in A minor!" Miss Bacon's fingers struck one chord, then another, going through several keys. Finally the boy sang a solo of his own choosing before she beat out a rhythmic pattern which the nervous auditioner duplicated.

At one point Calvin noticed that a student judge, perhaps only four years older than himself, stepped forward to harmonize with the new recruit. Other young judges, seated a short distance away, listened carefully to determine whether the candidate could hold his own part. Usually he did.

Calvin wondered, were the judges grading boys for how they reached for a note? Or for how much each knew about music?

He learned later that they had jotted down more than a candidate's pitch and response. They had added personal comments: "Lots of confidence, okay voice, good rhythm, very shy, and easy to get along with." Because the workload would be difficult, if a boy did not get along with others, how good would rehearsals be?

Calvin noticed that when Miss Bacon rejected a boy, she also invited him to try again the following year. He liked that.

Itching to perform, he fidgeted. Finally, when it was his turn he stepped forward. Walking boldly to the piano, he heaved a tiny sigh, and did what had never been done before. Using the piano pedals, with heavy chords he began to play his own music. His graceful, skinny fingers knew exactly where to go. In a raspy voice Calvin sang out with vigor. Years later he said of this day, "I honored them by playing one of my own compositions—a nervy thing for a nine-year-old to do. But Madi certainly noticed me!"

Indeed she did. She loved his self-confidence and recognized his extraordinary sense of music. "His voice was not terribly good," she said, "but he was a natural!"

Half in fun, Calvin shocked everyone at his first rehearsal. Parents and boys, used to Madi's discipline, stood by speechless as he banged out another set of original chords on the piano.

Despite this noisy beginning, Calvin found a second home in the San Francisco Boys Chorus, and a lifelong friend in Madi Bacon. Yet no one, not even Calvin, imagined that decades later he would bring music to millions of people.

- II -
Early Impressions

Calvin Eugene Simmons was born on April 27, 1950, at 10:11 p.m. in San Francisco's Mt. Zion Hospital. He was a much wanted child of older parents. His mother, Mattie Pearl, was a registered nurse and the choir director of the Mt. Zion Baptist Church. Calvin's father, Henry Calvin Simmons,* worked hard as a longshoreman and was the financial secretary of their church. Julia Dixon, Mr. Simmons' older daughter from a first marriage, lived independently in Los Angeles.

Calvin came into an era before anyone knew about CDs and VCRs. Only one in ten families owned a television set. Movies and radio provided home entertainment. People were humming such tunes as "If I Knew You Were Coming I'd Have Baked a Cake" and "Good Night Irene." Serious music lovers listened to radio's New York Philharmonic concerts conducted by eighty-three-year-old Arturo Toscanini.

Although Calvin's father did not play an instrument he loved music and often brought records home. Calvin liked to climb into his dad's lap and listen with his father to jazz, the classics and the popular stars—Elvis Presley, Peggy Lee, Dave Brubeck, Sarah Vaughn and Ella Fitzgerald.

He was a happy child. His parents trusted him, and unless he

---

*Since 1969, Mr. Simmons has been Chairman of the Board of the Mt. Zion Baptist Church.

lied, they did not spank. He sang and danced and was especially fascinated by the piano. Before Calvin was three, he was sitting next to his mother, fingering piano keys and picking out familiar tunes.

One Sunday morning Calvin made an unexpected debut in church. Before Mattie Pearl began to lead the Mt. Zion Baptist Church choir, she seated Calvin, as usual, alongside the chorus. But as she conducted she heard titters behind her back. Unable to turn around, she did not understand what was happening.

The amused congregation was watching her son. Calvin had jumped up and, standing directly behind his mother, was waving his arms in what he considered to be conductor style. Looking down after the hymn ended, Mrs. Simmons discovered her three-year-old grinning with satisfaction. What could she say?

Mattie Pearl began to carry Calvin to rehearsals when he was six weeks old. Choir members took turns bouncing him on their knees and their melodious voices lulled him to sleep. Music came as naturally to Calvin as breathing.

At home he watched his mother prepare for choir practice and as he grew older his eyes followed her hands on the piano keys. Soon he was imitating whatever he heard. Once when Calvin interrupted her practicing once too often, Mattie Pearl told her husband, "We're going to need two pianos in this house!" Two years later the Simmons's bought that second piano, a spinet, which they placed downstairs. Mr. Simmons sometimes found himself placed between music coming from upstairs and below at the same time.

One day when Mrs. Simmons caught Calvin scribbling on her sheet music, she asked what that was all about. He said he was marking sheets the way she did. Instead of scolding, she gave over her old music books for him to notate any way he wanted.

Calvin was almost four when the family drove to Louisiana to meet Mattie Pearl's relatives. Sitting quietly in the back seat of the car, he watched the passing scenery until just outside Shreveport. Then he threw one of his shoes out the window. He was trying, he said later, to feed a cow.

Only after Mattie Pearl began straightening his clothes did she discover the loss. So a one-sock-one-shoe son was handed into his grandmother's waiting arms, and Mattie Pearl's mother proudly paraded her only male grandchild before neighbors and friends. Everyone heaped him with hugs and kisses until, overwhelmed, Calvin finally asked, "Mother, why do they kiss so much down here?"

Mrs. Simmons told him what her preacher father had taught her "A friendly kiss is a holy kiss." Years after Calvin grew up, wherever they met—in London, Paris or New York—he always greeted close friends with hugs and kisses.

Calvin and his father were best friends. He loved the grits his father cooked, the secret talks they shared and the weekend strolls they took through the neighborhood. Sometimes they watched a sandlot baseball game or sailed a toy boat on Stow Lake in San Francisco's Golden Gate Park.

Like many boys, Calvin owned a collection of trains and trucks. Once he told his mother he might want to work on the docks like his dad or be a truck driver so he could travel around the world.

While his parents encouraged him to be true to himself, and Mattie Pearl liked to repeat, "You are who you are," she secretly hoped he would become a doctor. Thus, her response to his truck-driving ambition was firm. "There will be no truck drivers in this house. Who wants to sleep on the road?" she asked.

At five, Calvin announced he knew how to play piano. Taking him seriously, Mattie Pearl immediately played something, then asked him to duplicate it. To her surprise Calvin duplicated exactly what she had played. It was time she decided, for formal lessons and she would teach him herself.

The first sessions progressed well. But within months, Calvin was protesting, "Mother, that's an eighth note. You told me that!" Or, "You didn't hold that note long enough!" Arguments continued until Mrs. Simmons hired Mrs. Tilly Amner, a local piano teacher. Calvin later could not recall Mrs. Amner by name, but when he was eight, he played a Chopin piece elegantly in a church recital.

Bold as Calvin's approach to music was, a certain shyness at times showed through. Once in a neighbor's house, while Mrs. Janice Mickens prepared hamburgers for several youngsters, Calvin watched quietly. After the others asked for ketchup, one child said, "Calvin wants mustard."

"What kind do you want?" Mrs. Mickens asked. "I have all kinds, yellow, brown. Name it." "I'll take French's, thank you," Calvin said politely. Throughout his life, most people enjoyed Calvin's merrymaking. Only a select few sensed his more reserved, modest nature.

In school, Calvin liked to tell silly jokes to make his classmates laugh. Eleanor Segrue, principal at the Andrew Jackson Elementary in San Francisco remembered him as "a friendly boy with sparkling eyes, a beaming smile—just music himself."

Yet somehow his peers sensed that he was not quite like them. He wanted to make music all the time. When he heard a note, he not only knew its name; if someone said, "Sing me a G," he could do it almost perfectly.

"At music time when I used a one-hand-on-the-piano-keys technique, Calvin would pop up with 'Let me do it.' His musical ability was obviously better than mine," his third grade teacher Ms. Tapples said, "so I let him start the songs."

After school while friends played outdoors, Calvin usually practiced piano. He did not mind being alone, music made him tingle all over. If he finished early he joined in a neighborhood game. Sometimes however the boys teased him. In a whining voice someone would yell, "Here comes Calvin. Does he have his piano tucked under his arm?"

Though the words hurt he shrugged them off. He was who he was and he was comfortable with himself. What anyone else thought was of no consequence because he knew what he wanted to do. Soon those hours of practice in solitude paid off because he was asked to perform for the entire school.

Seated in the audience Mrs. Simmons glowed. Music, she knew, would always be important to her son. But like others, she never considered that Calvin might be applauded for performing on stages around the world.

(Below) Calvin, age 14, on tip-toes, leads the SFBC members in song.

- III -
The Woman Behind the Boys Chorus

It is difficult to imagine what Calvin's life would have been without the San Francisco Boys Chorus (SFBC). But one certainly knows that Boys Chorus would not have thrived without Madi Bacon.

Born on February 5, 1906, Madi Bacon grew up in a music-loving family. Her Wisconsin-born father was an obstetrician. Her mother was a direct descendant of Esterhazy aristocrats in Austria, who supported composers Franz Joseph Haydn and Franz Schubert. Her favorite brother, Ernst Bacon, became a respected American composer.

Tutored at home until the seventh grade, Madi entered school proficient in English and German and knowing a little French. She excelled in basketball, baseball, field hockey and swimming and practiced piano two hours every day. She wanted to become a conductor, but that was an impossibility for a girl born in the early 1900s.

Nevertheless, she studied conducting with Serge Koussevitzky, the renowned conductor of the Boston Symphony. Later as a teacher, Madi started performing groups wherever she lived. She led madrigal singers in Chicago, hospital and shoemaker choruses elsewhere in Illinois and, in Berkeley, taught extension music courses at the University of California.

In 1948 Maestro Gaetano Merola, founder and General Director of the San Francisco Opera, and his Choir Director, Kurt

Herbert Adler, asked Madi to select and train young boys from the city's schools to sing on stage with the opera company.

The boys performed so well that three mothers, Edna Holm, Ilse Wehm and Marie Zeller, set up a nonprofit organization to keep the chorus going after the opera season ended. Within two years Madi was training four groups nonstop. Half the boys lived in the East Bay, and their parents had to struggle to get them to rehearsals and performances on time. Over the years Madi broadened the repertoire to include madrigals, folk and sacred songs, and choral selections from forty-five operas. But the boys learned more than music.

In the beginning the Chorus operated on a tiny budget. Boys were expected to pay twelve dollars a month dues, but no one was turned away for lack of funds. By the time Calvin joined in 1959, the group had grown to between eighty and one hundred boys from diverse ethnic and religious backgrounds.

With parents chaperoning, the boys journeyed to sing regularly in Southern California, usually staying at the Hotel Figueroa in Los Angeles for one or two weeks. Because Madi did not tolerate lazy habits, the boys cleaned their rooms and did school work on the hotel mezzanine after breakfast. Parents reminded them regularly not to ride the elevator for fun or to have pillow fights in their rooms. Occasionally they did, but mostly they were, as Madi said, "Always well behaved." After rehearsals they swam, exercised, played games, or visited museums. These trips lasted from the late '40s into the '60s.

The boys appeared on an Ed Sullivan TV program and in the filming of an opera. They sang on radio, in San Francisco at parties for foreign consulates, and in Union Square. Once they entertained the king of Norway at City Hall and Adlai Stevenson and U Thant on United Nations Day.

The Opera paid only "reasonable expenses," so parents, friends and Madi did fund raising all the time. Even after she joined the opera company's musical staff, Madi never earned more than $10,000 a year, but what she gave the boys cannot be measured in money.

Madi worked with heart and demanded intelligent action. If she told a boy to "sing sweetly" or made the Chorus repeat phrases until they sounded right, they tried harder. She was their friend and they respected her orders. Bob Fahrner once told his mother, "Madi makes you know you can do things you didn't know you could do."

Calvin flourished in the Boys Chorus where his new friends nicknamed him "Fingers." He sang, he composed, told jokes and somehow managed to be where the action was. Because he could sight read notes and did everything musical easily, most people assumed he never studied. They were wrong. At home he practiced or listened to records constantly. Before long Madi assigned him to teach music theory or to accompany a group on the piano.

When he was almost thirteen Madi let him lead the boys through brief passages. But the funny faces Calvin made sent everyone into uncontrollable giggles and annoyed her.

One day Madi told him, "Look, the whole world knows you have a good sense of humor. Let's show the boys there's a serious side to you too." She asked him to learn a slow movement in Pergolesi's *Stabat Mater* and then warned him, "If you so much as chuckle out there, I'm going to kill you."

Stabat Mater is a complicated piece. Its solo parts call for a soprano, second soprano, and alto. The music expresses Mary's mourning for her lost son, Jesus Christ. Calvin tackled this assignment with solemn intensity and at performance time walked on stage with great dignity. Erect and ready, dressed in their navy blazers and grey trousers, the boys focused on him.

Immersed in the music and caught up in the religious mood of the boys' voices, Calvin stood on tiptoe. Curving his body into a big letter-like C he seemed to almost topple over. Nothing, probably not even an earthquake could have distracted him as he strained to bring out the best in his singers. Afterwards Madi said, "What a beautiful job you did." Thinking back years later, Calvin said, "Standing there...all these friends, leading them, watching them respond to you, with all of us in uniforms, it felt like one great big family."

By 1965 the boys were making one hundred appearances a year. The Opera staff referred lovingly to them as "our boys." While waiting in a dressing room below the stage, they met the greats of opera—Ezio Pinza, Leontyne Price, Kirsten Flagstad, Mary Costa and Marilyn Horne. On stage they sang in French and Italian. After they took part in a recorded performance of *Boris Godunov* (sung in Russian) with Leopold Stokowski conducting the San Francisco Symphony, a critic wrote that the Boys Chorus had become "one of the finest groups of young voices in the nation."

Every December the boys entertained at Berkeley's Southside Community Church and at Rotary and Kiwanis Club Christmas parties. Either Calvin or another boy led the songs, while others roamed the aisles handing out lollipops and balloons and carried two-and-three-year-olds up front. Adults and children sang and applauded, and everyone had a merry time.

When Austria's Vienna Boys Choir came to town, Madi's boys acted as their gallant hosts. At home these Viennese boys lived in a palace away from their families. Their education was funded by their government and private churches, and they studied academics, took voice and choral lessons and sang year round.

Although The Vienna Boys Choir approached singing differently than the way Madi taught, the two groups shared more than concerts. Whooping it up, they ate too many desserts, taught each other magic tricks (Calvin knew quite a few), played basketball, swam and sang for the fun of it. Only a few of the visitors spoke English and not many Boys Choristers spoke

German, but through the common languages of music and laughter, barriers toppled and some boys became good friends.

Calvin talked about Madi all the time. This petite woman who had trekked through Nepal, camped in Europe, South America and Africa, was the boys' conductor, teacher, coach, and friend. Today our country enjoys the music of hundreds of professional musicians from among her fifteen hundred alumni who started their musical life in Boys Chorus.

*Calvin's
camp
performances
were
unique!*

DICK MEYER

DICK MEYER

*(Above) Calvin hits a high
note during an aria from*
The Mikado.

*(Left) Calvin masquerades as
his life-long hero,
Wolfgang Amadeus Mozart.*

- IV -
The Impish Camper

Calvin loved city rehearsals, but he thrived even more on camp life at Feather River, near Quincy, California. At age eleven, lying on his cot he listened to the wake-up notes of Beethoven's *Pastoral Symphony* drift through the trees. Promptly at seven a.m. he joined others hurrying to the dining hall where the day began with simple prayers.

He and other boys thanked God for not letting it rain, for keeping someone's dog healthy at home, and for their good food. After a hearty breakfast prepared by the camp cooks, June Hall and Charlotte Jackson, the boys raced through a slap-dash cleanup before forming clusters around a half dozen rented pianos on the campground. Outdoors under trees, Calvin learned music theory, sight-reading, the history of music, and practiced choral pieces for the coming opera season.

Calvin's teacher-counselors, who received only room and board, were all musicians. Most excelled in sports, and the majority were Chorus graduates. Some taught in the city, and Madi always recruited several composers, including her brother Ernst, Jonathan Elkus and John Edmunds. These men wrote music and taught the more advanced boys.

For years William Duncan Allen, music critic and accompanist to the singer Todd Duncan (the original Porgy in *Porgy and Bess*) was Madi's assistant camp director. He taught Calvin music theory and also turned a cabin into an "Eagle's Nest," where older boys could listen and follow musical scores undisturbed. Calvin was one of his most frequent visitors.

After lunch the boys returned to their open-air, screened-in platformed quarters, where they read, wrote letters, drew or painted and listened to a counselor read aloud. But talking was taboo. Madi believed that "In the city boys are over-scheduled, always rushing somewhere. A boy needs time to reflect and understand himself," and she created space for that to happen.

Weekday afternoons Calvin did arts and crafts, hiked or hunted for quartz crystals and flecks of gold with Madi. Quite often, in blazing yellow swim trunks, he splashed and canoed on the river with bunkmates. Fascinated by trains, he often paused at dusk to watch the Western Pacific silver "Vista Dome" coming around the mountain.

Madi kept everyone active. Behind her back boys would sing, "Anything you can do, Madi can do better. Madi can do anything better than you," and they were not wrong. Madi could out-hike and out-ping-pong them all!

One memory many campers share was the day the temperature dropped to twenty-six degrees and the boys dressed in everything they owned. To keep warm, Madi organized a wood-gathering mission. "Pile the wood and we'll light fires," she said. Minutes after she lit the largest woodpile, a forestry fire truck with sirens screeching raced down the hill. After dousing the flames the forest rangers lectured a very subdued Madi, informing her that a permit was required by law for any kind of practice fire drill at any time.

The boys mostly avoided trouble and Quincy's citizens looked forward to their visits. The Choristers usually traded a concert for free rides and desserts at the summer Fair. Once after Bill Allen learned that the Fair animals would be gone before the Chorus sang, he arranged for a few creatures to be transported to camp to surprise Madi.

Let in on the secret, several boys detained her at a waterfront picnic. When she spied a llama, a three-and-a-half-foot-tall elephant and a clown trooping over the road, she was as someone said, "Knocked off her perch."

Before the animals trekked back to town, the clown told the boys, "This camp feels like home." And the boys responded, proudly, "It's not every day that an elephant joins our spaghetti feed!"

As Calvin grew older, everyone looked to him for the unusual fun. He set off peals of laughter at mealtime with just a wink or started the best water fights in the showers or at the washtubs. Somehow when he bent a rule, he got away with it.

The day Calvin developed a sore throat from the dust, he started a camp tradition. Wearing two sandwich boards that read: I AM NOT TALKING, he walked around silently to save his voice. From then on, whenever a boy had a hoarse throat he wore a similar set of signs.

After supper everyone met around a roaring fire, where different boys performed stunts, did magic tricks or presented puppet shows. Inevitably Calvin's act was a show stopper on skit nights.

While others might put a lizard in a counselor's sleeping bag, Calvin did his mischief on stage. Borrowing clothes without permission—a counselor's dress or a muumuu—using a mop for a wig, with a squinched up face he rattled off zingy lines, impersonating at least one staff member.

Once, after raiding Madi's clothesline, he tucked two grapefruits inside her sweater and placed her cap atop his head. Dangling an unlit cigarette from his lips, he then scooped up a fistful of dirt and in an imitation of Madi's gravel voice, praised the earth's beauty.

At fifteen Calvin wrote and performed his own short opera. While playing piano he changed hats, altered his pitch and sang every role. People still talk about the night he wore the cook's long dress and her feathered hat and sang the Queen of the Night's difficult aria from Mozart's *Magic Flute*, reaching in falsetto to an F above high C.

Each day closed with taps. One boy might play a flute solo, another a French horn, or a cabin of campers might sing taps, or a Brahms or Schubert lullaby.

Calvin loved everything about camp but cold water so whenever possible, he avoided his swimming lessons. Either he lingered with the younger campers, or he made himself useful in the office. There, he caught Peggy Fahrner's eye and they became fast friends.

Peggy Fahrner was a San Francisco Boys Chorus board member and the parent of a chorister. She and her husband Leslie, co-directed the camp for several years. Behind the scenes she comforted homesick boys, shielded shy ones and kept parents who wanted special favors for their sons away from Madi. Madi always said the camp would not have run smoothly without Peggy's leadership.

Sundays were reserved for rest. There were no rehearsals and wakeup was an hour later. After a sumptuous breakfast, everyone gathered for a "morning sing." Later in the day boys played at the waterfront or joined Madi and Peggy in a vigorous game of "Capture the Flag." Calvin was not the greatest player, but one camper remembered, "When he ran his spindly legs moved like the wind."

Sundays closed at sundown with Vespers on top of the ridge overlooking the river. As darkness blanketed the sky and stars appeared, boys gazed toward the pines on the opposite bank, some trying to recognize a seahorse, a bear, a mysterious creature in the silhouetted trees. Lying side by side on sleeping bags, the youngest boys rested their heads on a favorite counselor's lap.

Madi would give what seemed like a casual talk but which

was actually linked to a problem that had risen earlier in the week. "Here we are, black, white, Catholic, Protestant, Jew, Buddhist," she might say. "We are in this beautiful place without a roof overhead. Each of us thinks differently about God because we are different." These gatherings built a sense of respect and trust for one another and helped to deepen friendships.

Serene and quiet among his peers, Calvin felt life was glorious.

At 15, Calvin already expected to have a career in music.

- V -
Student Days

The minute Calvin heard Mozart's *Symphony No. 40 in G Minor* at San Francisco's Roosevelt Junior High, he was hooked. "What is this?" he asked.

Within days, he turned into Louise McTernan's "most perfectly attentive student" and changed her general music class into a beehive of music lovers. And Wolfgang Amadeus Mozart, the genius who played piano by age three and wrote scores by age six, became, as Calvin later said, his "lifelong hero. I was a little kid loving a little kid composer."

Calvin lived in a mixed neighborhood of African Americans, Germans, Asians and Irish. His school provided a chorus for girls, nothing for boys, and few youngsters cared anything about classical music. But with Calvin's help and his experience in SFBC, Louise McTernan soon changed attitudes.

Together they organized twenty-four boys into a chorus, with Calvin as its accompanist and conductor. Evenings at home, he began to experiment, trying to discover how a conductor blends a full orchestra of eighty instruments into a single sound. One night, in the privacy of his bedroom, standing before a mirror, he raised a baton and conducted along with a recording of Beethoven's *Fifth Symphony*. He became the orchestra, conductor and audience rolled into one. Later he joked, "That was my first concert...a *wonderful* performance. The reviews were great and the audience loved it."

Days whizzed by. Most afternoons he lingered after school in the music room. While Louise prepared lessons, he would put a record on, turn to the empty tiered seats and pretend to be leading live musicians. Purposely he mixed things up. Sometimes he extended his skinny arm or bent a finger gesturing for strings when woodwinds were called for. He motioned for a bass when a trumpet sounded or a violin became the notes from a horn. Afterwards he would double up, laughing at his mischief.

Louise sensed that Calvin's talent was huge and because she wanted him to learn a variety of instruments, she convinced the band teacher, Bob Giambruno, to teach him the French horn. Having good breath control, Calvin caught on quickly. For a short time he studied the double bass, but he said, "I may be tall but basses are *big*!" and Calvin had no intention of lugging one around.

Louise continuously introduced Calvin to other instruments. Knowing they were costly, she arranged for him to borrow a few for practice at home. One time when Calvin tried to combine an oboe with a horn, the oboe's reed flew into the horn and got stuck in the serpent-like tubing, with disastrous results. Next, Calvin tried the violin. With each instrument his skills improved.

Academically, however, Calvin was an average student. If he studied his grades were okay, but he concentrated only on what interested him. He read Shakespeare, worked hard for Louise, and was excited about world history. But after he handed in a late history report, his social science teacher kept him back a grade over other teachers' objections.

Calvin's parents soon after transferred him to Aptos Junior High. Still, he kept in touch with Louise and eventually became a frequent visitor to her home.

Meanwhile at Aptos, he continued to create new opportunities for himself. The day Joseph Alessi, the new music teacher, arrived, Calvin asked, "Can I conduct the band?"

"Do you mind if I conduct it first?" Alessi asked, realizing he was facing a "persistent kid."

Alessi had played trumpet with both the Metropolitan Opera and Philadelphia Orchestra and Calvin recognized that he was a master teacher.* So he pestered almost daily for permission to play the bassoon and to improve his conducting technique, until Alessi finally showed him how to sketch a score.

Alessi wrote the melody in yellow pencil, the rhythm in blue, and the harmony in red; then he gave Calvin an assignment which should have kept him occupied for a week. Three days later Calvin was back with a score. He closed the book and played the entire piece from memory. "This kid is good!" Alessi decided and lent him a book about conducting written by his former boss, the renowned Max Rudolf.

During lunch hours at Aptos, Calvin and his friends liked to make music in the bandroom. He had begun to compose, and for an original opera he playfully borrowed the term *meno-mosso* (which means slower or with less motion) for the character name "Mini-Mosso." He also wrote an anthem for the SFBC and a composition for flute, clarinet and trumpet, which his friends Ann Sheedy, Doug Tolliver and Bill Tull performed at graduation.

Often he practiced with Bill Tull at Bill's house. The same neighborhood boys who had teased him in the past now sat outside and listened to the duets. They realized that Calvin was as passionate about music as they were about sports.

Sometimes, after school he and Alessi played music together. Once their vice principal walked in. After listening to their session he arranged for them to present a school concert, which was greeted with wild applause.

The year Calvin entered San Francisco's Balboa High School,

---

*Today Joseph Alessi is the principal trombonist of the New York Philharmonic.

Joseph Alessi transferred directly across the street to City College. On opening day Calvin was at his door. "Don't you ever go to class?" Alessi asked.

"I don't care about grades. I want to conduct," Calvin replied. Once again he persuaded Alessi to let him help—this time at the college between his own classes. Then on Saturdays he assisted John Lam, the music teacher at Lowell High School, often accompanying the Lowell chorus at their concerts.

In the halls and in gym at Balboa, Calvin's quick, graceful stride and super energy attracted the coaches. He was a fast runner and they wanted him to race, but he would not run track. For Calvin there was only music, music all the way. He even agreed to play tuba for the jazz band, the one position open, because the tuba made it possible for him to travel to music festivals. One school buddy described the tuba um-pah-pah sounds he made as "strange bloated honks."

When Calvin wasn't with Alessi, he was underfoot in Balboa's music department. It wasn't long before he and Sidney Walker, the band teacher, became good friends. One choir student described Walker as "a strict man who was well loved because he took time to teach properly."

Like Louise, Walker recognized Calvin's "uncommon competence," and hired him to give piano lessons to his own children. Calvin was a mere five years older than his young pupils, and they loved him. Often he stayed on for supper and for vigorous political discussions with Walker.

Balboa's slogan at this time was "First on the Pacific," and Calvin achieved several firsts of his own. With Sidney Walker's support, he became the first student to play in both band and orchestra and the first to compose and conduct music. He even created special music for the school's modern dance classes.

Calvin spent most of his free periods in the bandroom where one female classmate remembers him as a "poor dresser and not particularly good looking. His one interest was band. He was quiet and just came to play the piano."

Calvin involved himself in everything musical. At the close of school, dressed in a blue denim apron much like one worn by violin makers in past centuries, he efficiently replaced the broken strings of the orchestra's violins.

In the 1960s, with the birth of the Civil Rights movement, black militancy was spreading across the country. At Balboa, those who wanted to voice their independence ridiculed anything European, including classical music. To them it lacked soul. But Calvin could not think in those terms. For him, music was universal, a language that expressed joy, sorrow, energy, love and pain. "If you love something...you won't clutter the mind with begrudging things," he said.

The 1960s were stirring years, and sometimes at Balboa some white and black students clashed. Those who wanted to avoid a bus fight stayed on school grounds. When Mrs. Simmons worried about her son, Calvin reassured her. "I'll be fine, mother." And he was.

Protective of his students, Mr. Walker let those he trusted meet in his small office. One day while "messing around," Calvin accidentally broke the mirror Walker used to demonstrate how to project a true voice.

"I want you to buy a new mirror," he told Calvin.

"I'm not going to pay for that," Calvin insisted.

"I want a new mirror tomorrow morning," Walker firmly repeated, "or you will find a new high school." And Calvin knew he meant it.

The next morning Calvin delivered a gift-wrapped mirror tied with blue ribbon, then mockingly dropped onto one knee. "Massa, oh Massa, don't whip me!" he joked. Calvin respected Walker's sense of fair play, and that clash of wills deepened their friendship.

Pushy as Calvin appeared to be about music, he was sensitive
to the needs of others. When he realized that Ned Hardin, his
music teacher, was seriously ill, he taught the class with Hardin's
approval. No one knew that Hardin had cancer until he died a
year after Calvin graduated.

Calvin loved children, and every year he planned a neighborhood special Halloween night for them. After decorating his
house with large carved pumpkins, he would put on a recording
of Mussorgsky's *Night on Bald Mountain* at full blast. Those
children who dared to knock at the Simmons' door were fright-
ened by a creature in a white sheet with an eerie painted face,
who then invited them in to enjoy treats and a round of scary
songs.

Around this time, Calvin's parents started a tradition of their
own. Because they wanted to become better acquainted with his
favorite teachers, they shared many Thanksgiving and Christmas dinners with the Walker family and the McTernans.

Wherever Calvin went he made music. In the homes of friends
he played piano and everyone sang. He not only worked with
Alessi and Walker, two afternoons a week, he rehearsed with
Madi and the Boys Chorus. One summer with a recommenda-
tion from a Boy Chorus parent, he worked at Berkeley's
Berkwood school.

What a bargain he was! For a salary of a dollar and a half an
hour and carfare, at fifteen he taught singing and instrumental
music to children in kindergarten through sixth grade. Betty
Helpern, the program director said, "This wonderful kid played
piano, set up a chorus and directed a highly original version of
Shakespeare's *King Lear*."

The next year, at sixteen, Calvin became choir director of
seventy youngsters at his Mt. Zion Baptist Church, a post he
kept until he left for college. That same year, Madi introduced
him to the highly regarded San Francisco piano teacher, William

Corbett Jones.

Calvin was not Professor Jones' best student. Busy as he was, he did not practice enough. But Jones remembered that Calvin did repeat the difficult Mozart *Sonata K284* many, many times until he played it with Mozartian grace. When Calvin was away at college, he telephoned Jones to tell him that he was the one who had shown him how to discipline himself. Jones, on the other hand believed that Calvin learned discipline in college where he encountered tougher competition.

Once when Calvin wanted extra money, he demonstrated toy organs in Woolworth during the Christmas season. But whenever he had an hour to spare, he headed for the San Francisco War Memorial Opera House. From his first visit, everything in that building—the architecture, the scenery, the vast stage, the singers, the musicians and the stars—impressed him.

Madi permitted him to sing in only two operas, Arrigo Boito's *Mefistotele* and Mussorgsky's *Boris Gudunov*. Still, he attended all rehearsals and at performance time was made up, costumed and ready to go on stage. He loved opera and just couldn't stay away. Quietly, he showed up when the Chorus wasn't even scheduled to perform. Dressed in his chorus sweater, he would slip past the unsuspecting doorman and keep out of people's way. Hiding in the folds of the heavy gold curtain on the left side of the stage, unnoticed, he watched operas night after night.

As he grew bolder, he asked musicians to lend him an operatic score or two, then conveniently forgot to return them for, as he said, "nine years." At school he told friends, "I am unable to keep my eyes out of scores. I study them all the time."

Eventually Madi made Calvin her Boys Chorus accompanist. One time, in the middle of a rehearsal, Calvin surprised everyone with an imitation of the opera's General Director, Kurt Herbert Adler. Seated at the piano, he placed a pencil in his mouth for Adler's pipe, then in a thick German accent told Madi,

"I must say your boys are doing a great job. One boy in particular is splendid."

"Who is he?" she asked, unaware that Adler had entered the room.

"I can't remember. What is his name? Collins Simpson or someone or other."

Everyone including Adler laughed. Many years later Adler said, "Calvin could imitate me perfectly, and no one was more entitled to do so than he."

Stagehands, set designers, voice coaches, musicians, all befriended this gangly youth with the easy laugh. As he became more visible, staff members asked him to substitute for a pianist on a "coffee break" or to coach several Western Opera singers. Calvin jumped at every opportunity. Learning from the ground up in this fine opera company was exactly what he wanted to do.

- VI -
The Camp Counselor

Calvin came to SFBC as a second soprano but his voice was never really good. In his teens he sang a fair alto. Madi always said, "His voice improved, but not much." She let him sing only one solo, the witch in *The Hypnotist*, and when he uttered a bloodcurdling scream, the audience gasped.

But Madi did not want to lose him. At fifteen, Calvin was too old to be a camper, not yet old enough to be a counselor. So she assigned him to kitchen duty. Calvin moved into the smallest camp cabin with Philip Kelsey, two other kitchen helpers and a litter of kittens no one was supposed to know about. The next year she made him her music assistant and sent the boys who needed special coaching to him.

Making tutoring sessions a mixture of fun and seriousness, he often suggested, "Get the jaw down. Let's find out what's the matter."

Tim Ericson remembered that at one lesson, Calvin began by playing a classical piece on the piano. Abruptly he stopped, started over and this time included every mistake a beginner might make. Later, when Calvin learned that Tim too admired Mozart, he lent him the score to Mozart's *Requiem* and never asked for it back.

Philip Kelsey, like Calvin, was an overaged "hanger-on." Two years older than Calvin, he was the more polished musician. Calvin, who usually skimmed through pieces and neglected technique, inherited the accompanist's job only after Philip left for Harvard University. Yet, as different as they were, they shared common interests. They both composed, played organ in their churches, loved to entertain at parties, and studied with William Corbett Jones. Long after their bunkmate years together, they remained friends.

Calvin did not become a camp counselor until he was seventeen. It happened the day he stood in Madi's home listening to her think aloud. "My only problem," she said, "is that I don't have a black counselor." The perfect opportunity had presented itself. Drawing himself up to his full height of six feet two inches, Calvin asked, "What about me?"

Madi later said, "He certainly wasn't the most efficient counselor in the world." Nor was he the best role model for the younger boys. Efficiency was not his strength. He loved music but he fooled around too much to suit Madi.

If he demonstrated how to roll a sleeping bag, invariably the roll opened. Out spilled toothbrush, comb, soap and washcloth. Still, when he assumed responsibility for the wake-up music, Calvin selected every record carefully, and on the last day at camp, everyone woke to the hottest pop music he could find.

Many campers remember the night Calvin encountered a bat. His boys were already asleep when a bat flew into their cabin. Half-awake, Calvin spotted it. Waiting for nothing, in pajamas he leapt out the door, down the steps and fell to the ground. His high-pitched screams brought everyone running. Much as he delighted in nature, bats were not included.

But Calvin loved overnight campouts. With Dick Meyer, a teacher and flutist, he usually supervised the eight-year-olds down on the beach opposite what the boys called the "White Cliffs." One summer their youngsters asked to cook breakfast by themselves, so Dick and Calvin crawled back into sleeping bags and stayed out of the way. Every few minutes a boy would nudge one of their bags, ask a question and return to his buddies. Calvin and Dick giggled as they heard their instructions being reinterpreted. Half an hour later, smiling boys presented a plate of flat, sandy eggs mixed with bits of shell, and Calvin nobly swallowed every mouthful.

After curfew the counselors met at the fireside to make their own music. The arts counselor, Mars Fletcher, remembered the night she played melody when Calvin joined her in a peppy *Chopsticks*. As she watched him crossing his middle finger over the next one, an unusual thing to do, she asked, "What are you doing with your finger?"

"Well, it works," he said, continuing to slide his skinny fingers everywhere.

Calvin was still composing music in private for his own pleasure. Once unfortunately, he showed a new piece to Philip, who felt he had to point out a flaw—an extra note where in his opinion it did not belong. Philip suggested a change, but Calvin, who did not take criticism well, walked off in a huff and never altered the piece.

During his first summer counselorship, Madi asked him to team with Larry Maisel on a production of *The Prince and the Pauper*. Larry, a fellow counselor, had written the libretto (story). Madi asked Calvin to write the music, so he enthusiastically created an intricate introduction and tucked a minuet into the middle of the show. He and Larry cast the roles and shared directing responsibilities. Madi coached the leads and Calvin accompanied on the piano. The production was so successful that operettas became a major camp activity every season thereafter.

Unintentionally, however, Calvin exasperated Madi and Larry. When they asked for a copy of the score to keep for those who might perform in future productions, "He kept putting it off," Madi said. She did not realize till years later that Calvin did not know how to write music formally. No one, including Madi, had trained him to write music down. Usually he improvised, rarely playing a piece the same way twice. He actually had done a remarkable job.

Poor Larry returned to college empty-handed. Instead of sending a score, Calvin mailed a series of letters which Larry has kept all these years.

In the letters, Calvin pretended that he and Larry were the great English team, Gilbert and Sullivan, composer and lyricist of *The Mikado* and *H.M.S. Pinafore*. Addressing Larry as William Gilbert, he signed off as Sir Arthur Sullivan.

In one letter he wrote, "I don't have to do *P & P* (*Prince and the Pauper*) you know!!! (That sounds like the name of a railroad.)" In misspelled German he added, "Nie tun Itch Trinken wein," which translated means, "I never drink wine."

Months later in a follow-up letter, he said:

"...I am 3/4s of the way finished (with the score) ...I will get *P & P* to you soon. I'm really having fun with it."

Then Larry received one final note which read:

"Dear Larry, Worried, aren't you?"

Calvin never did complete the score. Instead, Madi paid a professional pianist to help before the Chorus performed *P & P* the following winter season. Years later, Houghton Mifflin published the operetta in a textbook.

Calvin was a natural leader, the camp's imp and more. Peggy Fahrner fondly recalled the night Calvin imitated the famous conductor, Josef Krips. Moving with the music of a recording, when the orchestra hit powerful crescendos or swelling sounds, she saw Calvin's head shake exactly the way Maestro Krips' did.

"Calvin, I don't know whether you are going to be a comic or a serious musician," Peggy said afterward, "but one day I will have to pay to see you perform." Not too many years later her prediction came true.

- VII -
A Dream Comes True

Nothing pleased Calvin more than when in his senior high school year, Sidney Walker appointed him student director of the musical *Gypsy*, composed by Jules Styne, words by Stephen Sondheim.

Under Walker's loose guidance, Calvin selected and coached a cast of fifty and organized and conducted a "pit" orchestra of fifty of Balboa High's student musicians. The razzle-dazzle production with its songs, "Small World, Isn't It?" and "Everything's Coming Up Roses," was a smash!

The show played to sell-out audiences but it cost Calvin his mid-year graduation. He had missed too many classes, and his exasperated principal decided he needed another semester to complete the required work.

On the other hand, Sidney Walker believed Calvin had gained more from this hands-on experience than anything he could learn in a drama class. Calvin did not mind staying behind; another six months as Walker's apprentice felt fine to him.

At home he continued to study classical music on his earphones. Once, after conducting through a Mozart symphony, he said, "I felt as if time stopped. It was above everything." Perhaps because he admired Mozart so much, he stopped composing. He told a few friends, "All I was writing was bad Mozart, *very bad* Mozart." And that wasn't good enough for his high standards.

As usual, Calvin filled every day, racing from school to direct his church choir or to SFBC rehearsals. Sometimes Madi put him in charge of keeping the younger boys out of mischief. They might be rowdy with others but they respected him. Matthew Farruggio, a stage director with the San Francisco Opera, recalled the performance of Wagner's *Das Rheingold*, when "Calvin kept sixty little fellows under control. He had them ready to go on and off stage and disappear without a disturbance."

During the years when many teenagers worry about a social life, Calvin practically lived at the opera house. He liked to peek in and say "hello" to the musicians. In turn, they paid tribute to him by tacking a note on their door that said, "No one admitted except Calvin."

Regardless of the hour, after Chorus rehearsals ended, Calvin found reasons for hanging around. He said, "I stuck my nose into things and generally made a pest of myself." Actually the staff thought he was a wonderful volunteer.

Everything he had learned from his mother, Madi Bacon, Louise McTernan, Sidney Walker and Joseph Alessi began to reap returns. Opera conductors sometimes asked him to help singers warm up their voices. He became a familiar face even to General Director Kurt Herbert Adler, who attended every major rehearsal. A special rapport developed between them. Adler, amazed at Calvin's knowledge of scores and languages, recognized his genius and dubbed him "a *Wunderkind*" (wonder child) and began to guide him.

One day the opera company's artistic assistant, Richard Rodzinski, heard Calvin amusing himself at the stage piano during a rehearsal break of *Der Rosenkavalier*. Rodzinski asked him to try a few difficult passages from this Strauss opera. Calvin read through the music, then played it with gusto. An excited Rodzinski immediately persuaded Adler to hire him and said he would take full responsibility if Calvin didn't work out. Thus Calvin, still in high school and only seventeen, became the youngest salaried staff employee and the "baby" of the San Francisco Opera Company.

Traditionally, Adler always called a pre-season meeting where staff members introduced themselves. When it was Calvin's turn, surprising everyone, he set aside his usual lighthearted gaiety and said, "You'll never know how much finally being on the staff means to me. This has been a long-time dream come true." At last, he was where he felt he belonged.

A couple of months before Calvin expected to graduate from high school, Louise McTernan, Joseph Alessi and Sidney Walker each separately invited Dr. Albert Renna, the San Francisco Assistant School Superintendent of Music, to hear Calvin play piano in the City's Youth Orchestra concert. Directly after the performance, Dr. Renna suggested that Calvin audition for the University of Cincinnati Conservatory of Music.

Calvin practiced briefly, then quit because he did not believe he was ready. Alessi persisted, insisting Calvin had nothing to lose, so reluctantly he went to the tryouts. He played only one piece, and to his surprise, walked away with a college scholarship.

That night Calvin and his father discussed the future. Being a practical man, Mr. Simmons understood too well the obstacles his son would face in the world of classical music. Few black musicians played in symphony orchestras; fewer still reached the podium.

"If you don't make it there, will you be able to get into another career?" he asked.

Not make it! The idea had never occurred to Calvin. Skin color had nothing to do with making music. He knew he would be either a concert pianist or a conductor. Yes, it would be a challenge, but he said, "I won't be bogged down by any problems around me." That extra half year in school had not hurt at all.

Everything seemed to be coming up roses.

Twenty-four days before Calvin's eighteenth birthday, Martin Luther King, Jr. was assassinated on April 3, 1968. Calvin knew the "Savage Sixties" well. Television and newspapers kept the history-making Montgomery boycott, the battling students, the sit-ins and the faces of murdered civil rights workers before the public every day. Now, the one man who had inspired courage in millions, who had demonstrated the effect of nonviolence, was gone too.

Saddened by events, Calvin sprang into action. To reaffirm Dr. King's ideals, he organized a public memorial concert of Mozart's *Requiem*. He brought together several high school music teachers, his friends, Louise McTernan's friends and members of his parents' church, and rehearsed a large chorus and four soloists in less than seven weeks.

On June 30, 1968, with Philip Kelsey playing the organ, Calvin led an adult chorus in San Francisco's Third Baptist Church. For a brief moment, the music of his one hero, Wolfgang Amadeus Mozart, honored his other hero, Martin Luther King, Jr. and eased people's grieving hearts. The music also expressed the principles Calvin believed in.

- VIII -
In Cincinnati

Alone and on his own for the first time, Calvin wrote to Louise that the University of Cincinnati was deluxe, his room tourist class and the food ordinary. Quickly he involved himself in the Conservatory's multiple musical activities. "From the beginning it was absolutely clear that Calvin's talent was greater than anyone else's here," Professor Elmer Thomas said.

Slender and good looking, in 1968 Calvin was one of the two African Americans on the Conservatory's sprawled-out campus. Looking forward to meeting the only other black person, voice teacher Sylvia Lee, who had arrived the same semester, he walked into her class and introduced himself. Then he volunteered to be her accompanist and they naturally became good friends.

Whenever they strolled together, with Mrs. Lee's arm tucked under his and Calvin gesturing and talking loudly, they attracted much attention. Often Calvin stopped and with a straight face told those who stared, "Why, she's my mother."

One day Mrs. Lee introduced him to her colleague, Max Rudolf. Thus Calvin found himself facing Joseph Alessi's former boss from the Metropolitan Opera, the man who had written *The Grammar of Conducting*, the same book Alessi had lent him back in Aptos Junior High.

Max Rudolf, who was born in 1902, was a prominent conductor in Sweden and Germany until World War II. When he came to America, he served as principal conductor of the Metropolitan Opera for fourteen years. In Cincinnati he not only taught at the Conservatory, he was maestro of the Cincinnati Symphony. Calvin decided that he had to study with this man.

So one Saturday morning Calvin knocked boldly at Rudolf's door and asked for an audition. If he was nervous, it did not show. "What opera do you know?" Max Rudolf asked.

Calvin mentioned Mozart's *Don Giovanni*, and Rudolf handed him the orchestral, not the piano score. "All right," he said kindly, "play it for me."

Orchestral scores are complicated and can be intimidating. Pages filled with notes are at least fifteen inches long and each instrument has its own musical staff. There may be fifteen, twenty or more staves, and the conductor has to know how each note sounds.

Even before Calvin touched a piano key, he could hear *Don Giovanni* in his head. He knew the libretto and the story behind the opera's creation—how Mozart's wife kept her husband awake by feeding him and telling tales until he finished the overture the night before its debut. Now, under Rudolf's watchful eyes Calvin concentrated hard to interpret the music perfectly.

Rudolf listened carefully, then handed him a score he did not know. This too, Calvin played well and immediately Rudolf recognized Calvin's extraordinary talent. Years later, remembering that morning, Rudolf said simply, "Calvin played flawlessly."

Calvin attended a heavy schedule of classes—piano, organ, harpsichord, German, English and music literature, and because of his SFBC training, was skipped into a third year music theory class. Rudolf became his most important teacher and after classes he rehearsed with Rudolf's opera and Choral Union groups. Bubbling with pleasure, he wrote to Louise, "I am also accompanist for the Musical Theatre. Can you believe it? Already for money!"

Continuously he added to his activities. He assisted chorus classes and became an accompanist to Italo Tajo, a Conservatory professor and one of the popular opera stars at the Met. Before he reached his twentieth birthday Calvin conducted four student operas: Menotti's *Help, Help the Globolinks*, Menotti's *The Medium*, Mozart's *Don Giovanni*, and Humperdinck's *Hansel and Gretel*. On weekends he sometimes gave recitals in private homes.

Before Calvin left for Cincinnati, Ernst Bacon had given him three lessons in basic conducting and offered a few words of advice. "On the podium, eliminate show-off, flim-flam action. You are not a dancer. You are there for the music. Never stoop over. If you want something from the orchestra, be dignified."

Remembering Bacon's wise words, Calvin opened his mind to everything Rudolf offered. Every day he found reasons to stop at his teacher's home or studio, where he browsed among thousands of scores stacked wall to wall.

Rudolf provoked, counseled and encouraged. Echoing Ernst Bacon, he urged Calvin to trust his instincts. He taught him how to stand on the podium, how to hold a baton, and explained the finer points of rhythm and tones. He explained too why composers wrote what they did and showed Calvin how to help an audience listen to music emotionally. He also urged Calvin to find his own approach. Calvin became his devoted student and Rudolf became a supportive cornerstone in Calvin's life.

Calvin spilled over with news in letters to his parents and Louise. Because he was an irregular letter writer, Louise supplied him with stationery and stamps and so received more mail than almost anyone else.

Once he told her, "I'd advise you to keep all letters. They might come in handy when somebody decides to write my biography. RUDOLF IS FABULOUS!!!! A very enjoyable, extra talented Rubicund, (ruddy) a humorous German conductor."

He also wrote: "I shall be playing Puccini's *Il Tabarro*. Sparkling performance." Then he added, "I'll be coming home this summer. Of course I'll be traveling by train."

Calvin used any excuse to ride the rails.

Back in San Francisco, that summer at age nineteen he became both SFBC accompanist and camp counselor and again worked in the opera house. At summer's end, he and Philip Kelsey chose to return to college across Canada via train. Young and curious, they interrupted the five-day journey to sightsee in Vancouver. Back on track again, they watched the passing scenery, slept, and Calvin read *Dracula*, his favorite book of the moment. (At camp he had dressed in a plastic poncho, worn a mouthful of fangs and raced through the grounds frightening everyone.) He left the train at Cincinnati; Philip continued on to Boston.

To celebrate his twentieth birthday, on April 27, 1970, Calvin boarded the famous "California Zephyr," and from the train wrote Louise, "I had a wonderful birthday and am hereby officially twenty years old, a nice round number."

A month later he scrawled a long message:

"On July 5th, I shall be playing with (are you ready?) the Cleveland Symphony at the Blossom Festival in Cleveland. I'm still in shock...but it came rather simply. Ben Snyder...General Manager of the Symphony's summer festival, phoned me out of the blue three weeks ago. He asked if I'd like to play a (piano) concerto. Tuesday last, I went to Cleveland and talked to different people. By the way I met Szell. (George Szell was the Cleveland Symphony conductor.) He's a very nice man despite popular belief. Szell will not be conducting. The assistant Michael Cherry will." Calvin continued, "I will play...that warhorse, the *Grieg Concerto*, but I'd play MacDowell with that orchestra." (He meant he would play anything with this beautiful orchestra.)

Enthusiastic as Calvin was before the concert, afterwards he realized he hated to perform. He said, "I've done something I don't feel secure about. I'm really shy. I hate being a soloist. I can't stand people looking at me. At least as a conductor my back is to the audience." But he did not have to worry. A few weeks later, Kurt Adler invited him to join the Merola Opera Program and Calvin's life changed dramatically.

Mr. Adler established the Merola Opera Program in 1957 in honor of Gaetano Merola, founder of the San Francisco Opera. Wanting American singers to have the opportunity to study and be "showcased" in their own land, he developed the first comprehensive program in the United States. Since 1957, over five hundred highly qualified singers and coaches have auditioned yearly in the larger metropolitan cities. Over a ten week period, the selected twenty or twenty-two *Merolini* (a nickname of affection) receive specialized training from June through mid-August in the San Francisco opera house.

Singers are coached in voice, diction, acting, movement including fencing, and techniques for applying stage make-up. They study languages and take private coaching with opera "greats," among them Régine Crespin, Leontyne Price, and Elisabeth Schwarzkopf. They sing publicly in two fully-staged operas and concerts and, in fall and winter, many tour with Western Opera Theater. Those who later become "Adler Fellows" perform in major productions with the main opera company.

As a vocal coach, Calvin too learned languages and the art of accompanying a singer's *recitative*, a freely delivered musical style of phrasing words. He helped singers pronounce words correctly and demonstrated how to reach for high notes without sounding as though they were "chewing bread." He also prepared the opera chorus and soloists before they rehearsed with the orchestra. Ignoring stagehands who might be moving trunks or dismantling scenery, he focused completely on what needed to be done at all times. Once, at a rehearsal he pounded piano keys with such force that he broke a finger, then laughing, played on.

His first major assignment was to rehearse the orchestra for Mozart's *Così fan tutte*. Backstage during the performance, he played a gong, the bells and whatever else was called for.

In the fall, when classes began again in Cincinnati, Calvin learned that Max Rudolf was transferring to Philadelphia. He had been invited to start a new opera department at the historic Curtis Institute, and Mrs. Lee was going with him. She in turn asked favorite students, Calvin among them, to audition for this unusual school.

Calvin knew he had to follow his friends, so one night he arrived home in San Francisco without warning. As he put his key in the door lock, Mrs. Simmons called, "Calvin, is that you down there?"

"Yes, mother, and we have to talk," and he and his parents talked late into the night. "What do you think?" he asked his dad. "I'm only a telephone call away," Mr. Simmons said softly. The next morning they called Mr. Adler. Because he agreed with Calvin's decision, Mr. and Mrs. Simmons gave their consent.

His transfer disturbed University of Cincinnati officials, so Calvin wrote to John Watson, Dean of the School of Music, explaining his need "to specialize in piano and conducting . . . (to have) experience with Eugene Ormandy, Leonard Bernstein, Daniel Barenboim, Maria Callas . . ."

Years later, Calvin told a reporter, "The telephone bills that first year were out of sight! But Curtis was the fastest two years of my life!"

- IX -
The Fastest Two Years

Curtis Institute offered Calvin everything he wanted. In Cincinnati, he had been one among nine hundred students. Here he studied with fewer than two hundred in small classes of four or five peers at most, and his teachers were master musicians.

Calvin loved the Institute's elegant furnishings, the polished wood floors and thick Persian rugs in huge rooms, which he considered comfortable and "homey." On several occasions he was seen sliding down a smooth wood staircase bannister that led into the oak-paneled meeting room, just because it was there. Usually he landed at the fireplace where he said, "I lay flat out like a frog set-up for a biology exam."

Curtis *is* a rare institution. It was founded in 1924 by wealthy, warm-hearted Mary Louise Curtis Bok Zimbalist. Because she believed talented music students deserve the best teachers, she provided them. "All I have done is give away the money my father earned," she said humbly. Actually, her instructors built a school with a sterling reputation.

Hundreds of young musicians from many nations compete for admission each year. Those who are accepted receive a full scholarship and superb training; eventually, many alumni share their music around the globe.

Among the most famous have been: Gian Carlo Menotti, the Italian composer of *Amahl and the Night Visitors*; the late Ameri-

can composer-conductor of *West Side Story* and *Candide*, Leonard
Bernstein; American opera star Anna Moffo; and Nino Rota,
Italian composer of the music for the film *The Godfather*.

At Curtis, Calvin could hardly contain himself. If classes began at nine, he started practicing piano at eight. He spent hours
among the library's collection of thirty-five thousand books, original manuscripts and letters. He listened to old fashioned and
long-playing records. He viewed films of operas produced by
the Institute and worked from original scores. Learning melodies
written for baroque instruments more than a century ago gave
him incredible joy.

Jazz, rock, classical and modern—Calvin savored it all. He
thought about how the piano limited sound to ten fingers and
dreamed about creating miraculous music with strings, woodwinds, brass and percussions in a full orchestra.

Time flew. Assemblies, concerts, recitals, lectures—Calvin attended everything. He participated in Bach chorales and operas
by Mozart. He led the student orchestra and was the piano
soloist when Leonard Bernstein visited and conducted, and he
never missed Saturday mornings when the legendary Eugene
Ormandy, conductor of the Philadelphia Orchestra, directed
Curtis students.

Calvin adapted to every situation. Once, when a blown electri-
cal fuse left the orchestra pit in darkness during a performance of
Mozart's *Così fan tutte*, undisturbed, he calmly played the harpsichord from memory.

Despite a heavy schedule, he kept in touch with Louise. Writing about an illness, he told her,

"I had funny looking spots on the back of my throat. Also
my glands were swollen. Therefore the doctor took it upon
himself to take blood tests. Several!!!!...Right now I feel
superb, so I hope his final prognosis... will be good. He is
also very expensive! *Mon Pauvre Banque.*" (My poor bank.)

Describing a short siege of homesickness, Calvin continued, "I'm suffering from a touch of nostalgia. I've never really had it this bad before. I'm sure I'll get over it. When do I get a goody package? Don't you realize I'm a poor starving student? (Believe me there is a lot of truth behind this statement!!!) Send help. Goody things: old shoes, a book on Lithuania, ant farms, Milton Bradley games, anything, just send!"

Then he added,

"I checked out two books that I think you will never picture me checking out: *Mein Kampf* and Herman Hesse's *Peter Camenzind*! My philosophy is 'Expand the mind as long as it's expandable.'"

When Calvin arrived, Rudolf Serkin was Curtis' sixth director. Born in Bohemia (Czechoslovakia), Serkin had made his debut with the Vienna Symphony Orchestra when he was twelve and studied with composer Arnold Schoenberg and Maestro Arturo Toscanini. Before and during his directorship at Curtis he gave recitals throughout the world. He was the founder of the Marlboro Summer Festival and the Marlboro School of Music in Vermont. And, in 1963 he received the prestigious President's Medal of Freedom for his outstanding service in America.

Mrs. Zimbalist once said, "Any place where Rudi has been is better for his having been there," and Serkin's students and Calvin agreed.

Drawn to Calvin's obvious talent, Serkin soon adopted him as his protege and invited him into his family. Mrs. Irene Serkin spoiled him with homemade cookies, hand-knitted sweaters and a scarf and played violin and piano duets with him.

Many Curtis alumni remember the afternoon Serkin and Calvin made a grand entrance to the weekly student-faculty tea. Everyone except Mrs. Serkin gasped when the pair tumbled down the broad staircase arm in arm. Without turning to see the pratfall, she said casually, "Oh, that's only Rudi and Calvin."

Much as Calvin admired Serkin, he adored Max Rudolf. To Calvin, Rudolf was a "walking encyclopedia." He knew everything about Mozart. In class, with wit and wisdom he nudged his students forward. "Big Max" (the name Calvin gave him) understood each pupil's moods.

One day after Calvin conducted badly, Rudolf called him aside. A let-down could happen to anyone, but Calvin had a responsive mind and a good ear. What was the problem?

Rudolf noticed that Calvin was often nonchalant and did not take himself seriously. So he told him directly, "You must feel you are important . . . Don't be flippant. Conducting is a serious business." This counsel, similar to Ernst Bacon's advice, set Calvin back on track. Soon after, he wrote Louise: "Serkin is a gem. But God bless Max Rudolf . . . He's a fountain of knowledge. If I am to become a *Great Conductor* it will be due to his mentorship!"

Celebrities often taught master classes during the Curtis school year. The day opera diva Maria Callas arrived in a bright red skirt and matching cape, black boots and a large hat, she spied Calvin as she stepped from her car. "Boy!" she said, "Take my bags."

"I am not your boy. I am your accompanist," he responded softly. Yet in spite of her blunder, after a few days he considered Callas both temperamental and marvelous.

Despite his tight budget Calvin managed to attend most local concerts and operas. But having spent half his life near or on the stage, he listened to performances with a critical ear. He once described the Lyric Opera company to Louise as "the worst in the world." He wrote:

"The soloists in the production of *Aida* were awful. Only Beverly Wolff . . . was a smash hit. The chorus was hideous. You could hear the organ playing to keep them in tune. And the staging looked like something for a 49er halftime show . . . It was bad!"

On the other hand, he raved extravagantly about what he liked. The first time he heard the young English cellist, Jacqueline Du Pré play, he wrote:

"Du Pré is absolutely fantastic . . . what a gorgeous sound. With a pianissimo (softness) that is out of this world."

Ms. Du Pré, who made her debut in London at age sixteen, won fame early. Unfortunately twelve years after Calvin heard this recital, she developed multiple sclerosis and had to abandon the cello.

About her husband Daniel Barenboim, Calvin wrote:

"Big Danny's Haydn was elegant, so superbly played by his orchestra that I hope never to hear it played better. EVER."

But about Barenboim's conducting of a Brahms piece, Calvin had something else to say.

"The Brahms was a bit too youthful but good. This supports my theory that Brahms should not be conducted, or pianistic-wise, played before the mature age of 30, *at least!*"

Daniel Barenboim was born in Buenos Aires, Argentina. His family settled in Israel when he was a child, and his parents were his only music teachers. He gave his first piano recital at age seven and made his debut as a conductor in Haifa eight years later. As a youngster he appeared as a pianist in Vienna, Rome, Paris, London and New York and recognition came swiftly. After 1962, he turned to conducting and he and his cellist wife toured and recorded extensively. In the 1970s he conducted operas throughout Europe. Today he is the music director of the Chicago Symphony Orchestra and general director of the Staatsoper Berlin.

Barenboim was twenty-eight and Calvin only twenty when he and Calvin met. After Calvin learned that they both enjoyed cigars, he told Louise, "He's still a child like me!" They became good friends.

Some of Calvin's letters contained less news and more hints for favors. Once before the winter holidays, he wrote:

"Now hear this, speaking about Christmas presents, I've found the answer. A $79.99 *GARRARD* turntable (4 speed) AM/FM Multiplex Receiver and two bookshelf speakers. An absolutely fabulous buy on sale here. Contributions to help the cause will be accepted *immediately*. Sale ends Saturday night Dec. 12th! . . . Reply soon."

Louise sent more than a contribution. She bought him the phonograph.

Calvin raced through Curtis days. He shared the podium with Big Max for an all-Mozart concert and wrote, "Yes, yes, he (Rudolf) liked my Mozart." He conducted the school symphony and accompanied at vocal recitals. He prepared singers and accompanied at performances of *Così fan tutte* and Handel's *Rodelinda*, and with each project his skills and confidence grew. Sharing a surprise with Louise, he wrote, "At a matinee performance photographers from *Opera News* were present. They took pictures of me...conducting, tuning the harpsichord, giving last minute instructions to singers." He liked the attention but did not let this publicity go to his head.

When Calvin first came to the Opera House, Kurt Adler intimidated him. But as he jumped into activities, even between semesters, a unique palship sprung up between them. Calvin began to think of Mr. Adler as his second father, and years later he insisted Adler was the man most responsible for the success that came to him.

The summer before Calvin was to graduate from Curtis, Mr. Adler appointed him assistant director of the Merola Program, and so at twenty-one he joined Adler's master class. Seated at a piano on a raised platform he had to anticipate whatever Mr.

Adler wanted, while below, seated behind a music stand on a high stool, Adler gave voice instruction to the Merolini. They worked well together.

Mid-summer, Adler increased Calvin's duties. One Sunday afternoon in July he led a concert version of *Don Giovanni* in Sigmund Stern Grove and afterwards declared, "There was nothing like it!" Shortly thereafter Mr. Adler offered him a full-time job—assistant conductorship with the main opera company. Calvin was touched, but wanting to graduate, he turned the job down.

Adler was furious. For the next few weeks he passed Calvin by in silence. One day they met at the elevators and as though still in the middle of the same conversation, Adler asked, "Well, if you go back to school and finish, then will you join the company?"

The answer was obvious. Calvin spent his last year at Curtis knowing what would follow. Four months later, on December 16, 1972, he made his formal debut conducting *Hansel and Gretel* in San Francisco's Palace of Fine Arts. His father and Mr. Adler, watching their "maestro kid" from backstage, beamed with pride.

In June at the Curtis graduation ceremony Calvin received the third annual Kurt Herbert Adler Award for outstanding musical ability. He used the $1,250 to travel and study in Europe.

In England, Rudolf Serkin introduced him to Otto Klemperer, the conductor about whom Calvin said, "I devoured (his records) because of those moving crescendos." Later on postcards, he wrote,

"England is such a great place but somebody must tell these people that they drive on the wrong side of the street."

Then after visiting Mozart's home in Salzburg, Austria, he told Louise, "I can't begin to tell you what it is like just being in the city of my God and patron saint." And Vienna held one more thrill.

In town less than an hour, as he waited to cross a street, Calvin realized Philip Kelsey was standing next to him. "What are you doing here?" they shouted simultaneously.

"I'm here on a music fellowship," Philip said and invited him to share his flat. During the next few days they played scores, sang arias loudly, laughed and joked, went to concerts and visited private inns, where they tasted newly pressed wine and listened to Gypsy songs played on a zither. Then they went their separate ways.

And so at twenty-two, Calvin had graduated from college, earned an award, made his debut as a conductor and visited Europe. He was ready to work full-time in San Francisco's opera house.

- X -
Maestro Kurt Herbert Adler

Calvin spent almost all his waking hours in the San Francisco Opera House. Daily, he bounded through its narrow halls past clutter and scenery, down the winding stairs to the below-stage dressing rooms. Occasionally for fun, he crossed the marble-floored lobby and leapt atop the foyer's marble table to strike a pose, then he went casually about his business. Once in a while he surprised a colleague by doing a pratfall outside her office, and he made it a habit to pop into the wig-making shop for afternoon tea. One gala evening he twirled and waltzed a friend down the hall to a special reception.

Playful? Yes, but beneath those antics, Calvin was serious and organized. The musicians and Mr. Adler enjoyed Calvin's humor and respected his immense skills. When Calvin received his first decent paycheck, he celebrated by purchasing season opera tickets for his mother and Louise McTernan. Then he treated himself to a dark blue BMW automobile, which he promptly called Amadeus, in honor of Wolfgang Amadeus Mozart.

Frequently he named Mr. Adler as one of the most important persons in his life. He loved working with him and said it was from him that he learned "not to do [work] for money."

Kurt Herbert Adler came to the San Francisco Opera as its chorus director and conductor. Born in Vienna, Austria, on April 2, 1905, the son of a wealthy manufacturer, he conducted his school orchestra at fourteen, and during his teens met the composer Richard Strauss. He studied music, drama and philosophy at the Vienna Conservatory, and straight out of school became assistant to the German theatrical producer Max Reinhardt. Later at Salzburg, he worked for Arturo Toscanini. He left Austria joining the Chicago Opera Company just before Hitler and the Nazis overran Europe. Five years later, in 1943, Gaetano Merola invited him to San Francisco because he believed "Germans are prompt, orderly and reliable." Adler's skills were greater than that. He was a showman, a scholar and a visionary.

Nine years into his San Francisco Opera career, Gaetano Merola died in Sigmund Stern Grove while leading "Un bel dí," his favorite aria from Puccini's *Madama Butterfly*. Adler stepped to the podium and conducted what became a memorial to the Opera's founder. Then he took command of the opera's complex organization, and over the next twenty-eight years, reshaped the American opera scene.

Maestro Adler masterminded everything at the Opera House. When he was not available, he sent scouts who checked all details throughout the building and reported back to him. When something went wrong, he reached the spot with uncanny speed.

Adler in German means "eagle" and bird-like, he swooped down on the tiniest flaws. Nothing escaped his sharp eyes. He checked the scenery, costumes, musicians, choristers and soloists. He corrected smeared make-up on a chorister's face and found the overlooked name tape showing on the sole of an extra's shoe. After he spotted a small tack from clear across the stage, at a later ceremony his stagehands presented him with a gold tack encased in lucite.

Once Adler noticed a star wearing polished fingernails in an opera of an earlier century. "No one wears nail polish in my performances," he told her curtly and sent her off stage.

When Rossini's opera *La Cenerentola* (Cinderella) called for splashing water and the Company operated with a stringent budget, Adler ordered the stage crew to improvise. So, at the suggestion of stage director Jean-Pierre Ponnelle, during performances water "rained" on stage through a garden hose punched full of holes.

Madi Bacon remembered the night Adler stopped her, put his arm on her shoulder and removed her pendant. "Do you mind?" he asked. That evening the diva wore Madi's cluster of diamonds on stage, and Madi's neck was bare.

Adler pioneered at least one new opera a year, and as the repertoire grew, so did the staff. As many as six hundred employees worked at times on a single production. Many of the operas Adler introduced have since become standard productions in other American companies.

As Adler's reputation grew, the City's wealthiest patrons became his staunch supporters. The season's opening night became the most glamorous event of the year. Adler was manager, talent scout, conductor and grand impresario. He cheered his big stars, coddled the temperamental ones and guided the debuts and careers of many: Marilyn Horne, Leontyne Price, Birgit Nilsson and Luciano Pavarotti and others, long before the world considered them superstars.

Everyone addressed him as "Mr. Adler" or "Maestro" and all except Calvin, obeyed the sign outside his door: PLEASE DO NOT ENTER UNANNOUNCED. Whether Adler was crusty cold or sweet as strudel, things had to be done his way. He was *the boss*—demanding, tough and often inflexible. He expected his staff to work as hard as he, and they did.

Calvin loved every challenge Adler set up for him. "I had to play [the piano] as though I was a seventy-piece orchestra...to understand the score as though [Mr. Adler] was conducting it." He also had to be ready to step in and conduct on a moment's notice.

Much as he admired Adler, when Calvin worked with a cast,

he preferred to be a healer. He could, if he had to, be a taskmaster. But usually if things went wrong, he tried to change moods with compassion and laughter and to coax stars into giving their best.

After watching one cast argue furiously among themselves about Richard Strauss's *Der Rosenkavalier*, he played the score, matching the music's tempo to the singers' rising voices. Suddenly everyone realized what Calvin was doing and felt foolish. Emotions cooled and the rehearsal continued.

Superstar Birgit Nilsson only agreed to sing in the *Fol de Rol* because she knew Calvin would be her accompanist. The *Fol de Rol* is the annual lighthearted, Opera fund-raiser. Until recently it was held in the Civic Auditorium. Wealthy San Franciscans in formal evening dress dined at candlelit main floor tables, while in the balcony other music lovers sipped wine and nibbled paté and cheese. Beginning at eight, everyone enjoyed two hours of arias, comedy, ballet and rock music. Afterwards people danced on the lighted circular stage until early morn.

In the 1973 *Fol de Rol*, Calvin came on stage wearing red socks and a Dracula costume. Playing a fast boogie beat, he turned the crowd into immediate hand clappers and gigglers. Later, he and opera star Beverly Sills appeared in a skit, she acting as an uppity prima donna, while he impersonated Mr. Adler. Ms. Sills laughed so much she could not stay in her part. Together they stole the show.

Mr. Adler's musical career as a producer-conductor spanned fifty-three years and, during more than half of those years, he built the Opera Company into a magical empire. It was the longest directorship in opera history.

Adler's Merola Program was a "first" in the United States. Ten years later he created Western Opera Theatre, and in 1975 he launched the lunch-hour free Brown Bag Opera Program, and the next year he introduced the American Opera project. Every new venture brought opera to many people who may have imagined that it was not for them.

Mr. Adler was active on many music boards, among them the National Council of the Arts, the International Association of Opera Directors and the National Endowment for the Arts. He received numerous awards, including the St. Francis of Assisi Award in 1973; and Opera America honored him in 1981 as "Dean of American Productions."

Calvin considered himself fortunate to be working with his friend, an inspirational genius who trained him as no one else could have.

Opera staff applaud Maestro Kurt Herbert Adler and Calvin as they pass through the wig room enroute to the "pit" for a performance of Lohengrin.

- XI -
Traveling With Western Opera Theater

One year after Calvin joined the opera company, Adler made him associate director of Western Opera Theater (WOT). Now he both conducted in the opera house and toured with the Merola singers and a stage crew.

During 1972 he, the cast, and a stage crew traveled to New Mexico, Utah, Montana, Oregon, Wyoming, Nevada and throughout California. They sang for Navajo Indians in Arizona, and for pipeline workers in Alaska, presenting shortened operas in English to sixty-three thousand people in fifty-nine cities.

Portable scenery was sent ahead by truck and station wagon. Local children often met the truck and helped unload, and the crew of men and women stagehands set up quickly.

Once, before performing at a rather rough school, Calvin overheard the principal tell the students, "If any of you move, you're gonna be thrown out of the room." His youthful audience responded with boos and spitballs. "I knew I had to figure something to do so they wouldn't kill me," Calvin said, "so I walked out limping." Sympathetic to his disability, the teenagers gave him their rapt attention.

The day WOT was to entertain at "Many Farms"—a Navajo Indian reservation in Arizona—Calvin noticed that older people filled the front of the auditorium while students sat in the less expensive rear seats. A wide middle was empty. Calvin waited and would not start the music until the students were permitted to move forward.

When WOT traveled by bus, Calvin usually sat in the second seat behind the driver. Sometimes he clowned or became a tour guide, commenting on sights along the road. If he wanted privacy, he wore earphones. His unspoken message was, "I am incommunicado." During the drive between cities he studied new scores. Although everyone teased him about those earphones, he enjoyed his "Walkman" and was just a few years ahead, using the invention which has caused a worldwide trend.

From the tour, Calvin once wrote Max Rudolf, "I am quite busy making music all over the country, and will always be grateful to you for keeping an eye on me and sticking me occasionally! Please believe me when I tell you that you're one of the closest...people to me. Not because of your superior musicianship, but because of your *rare* warmth."

Living with each other for several weeks at a time, company members became close friends. Calvin and William (Bill) Wahman became buddies in Santa Barbara. Calvin loved a joke and when they performed, sometimes he tried to throw Bill off balance by changing the *cadence* (the beat), or adding extra blues notes where none was expected. But Bill always caught onto his tricks.

Between tours they gave recitals together. At one late night rehearsal, Bill tried to tell Calvin tactfully how to behave on stage. "Please don't defer to me," Bill said. Giving Bill an icy stare, in a furious voice Calvin responded, "How dare you tell me how to take a bow!" He started to leave, but Bill gently coaxed him back.

Calvin played the piano and Bill sang *Lieder*, the art songs that express joy, sorrow, love and tragedy. Praising them, critics described Bill's voice as velvety and inspiring and Calvin's playing as elegant. Years later, remembering those days, Calvin said, "We just loved to sing and make music together. I've never had that feeling with other artists in my life."

Kurt Adler believed that most people would enjoy operas if they could see them, so he expanded programs, sending his singers out to where people worked and lived. They performed in shopping malls, parks, hospitals, factories and senior centers, and in 1973 Kurt Weill's *Threepenny Opera* was presented on eight different street corners in San Francisco. David Ostwald, a former Boys Chorus counselor, staged the musical, and Calvin conducted in top hat and tails. *Threepenny Opera* was a traffic stopper. Pigeons disappeared and crowds listened behind roped-off sidewalks. Afterwards Calvin said happily, "People sat on curbs and applauded wildly."

One day Calvin originated an event of his own. Rushing into Mr. Adler's office, he asked, "Why isn't Mozart's birthday being celebrated?"

"Why not?" Adler thought and immediately put Calvin in charge.

On Monday, January 27, 1973, Mozart's 217th birthday, Mayor Joseph Alioto declared Mozart Day in San Francisco and Calvin's well organized musical marathon ran from noon till midnight in the city's Curran theater.

The program included Calvin's former teachers William Corbett Jones and William Duncan Allen, pianist Peter Serkin [the son of Rudolf Serkin and who has since become a famous pianist] and the SFBC. Bill Wahman sang *Lieder*, Calvin played four handed piano with Robert Jones and Western Opera members sang. He even persuaded the esteemed Elisabeth Schwarzkopf to sing. Best of all, he convinced everyone to perform without salary.

Early in the program, just as William Allen was beginning to play a minuet Mozart had written at age five, the audience heard a loud thump. Calvin picked up the broom that had fallen behind the curtain and shuffling across the stage, pretended to be a sweeper. The crowd loved his action. A Mozart Festival has since become an annual San Francisco event.

This first Mozart celebration happened between road tours. Traveling taught WOT singers flexibility. Long bus rides, waiting in airports, sleeping nightly in different hotels, even staging was not easy. Sometimes a stage was not wide enough and scenery did not fit. Or because there were no dressing rooms, singers changed costumes in gyms, classrooms or behind a curtain. Everyone missed family and friends. Eventually pressures drained energy and some performances became sloppy, yet Calvin always expected a peak performance.

Jacqueline Benson remembers being so exhausted that she added extra notes one night where none belonged. After the first act of *Turn of the Screw* ended, Calvin came backstage singing her role exactly as she had done it. "What was that?" he asked. That was all he had to say and she improved. Calvin rarely gave a compliment but nights later after Jacqueline sang her major aria in *La Traviata*, he bowed and kissed her hand, and she knew she had won his approval.

No one ever forgot the WOT Alaska thirty-two-day statewide tour. The cast traveled by bus, seaplane, snowmobile, and even dogsled to bring opera to thirty thousand Alaskans. They performed four operas, Rossini's *Barber of Seville*, Verdi's *La Traviata*, Krenek's *What Price Confidence* and Bernstein's *Trouble in Tahiti* in communities from Anchorage (population 150,000), to Kivalina (population 195).

Calvin's friend, Ann Seamster, was tour director, and she kept everyone moving on schedule. Calvin liked to stand beside her, and as she tapped her foot, checked her watch, glared at latecomers and checked her watch again, he would imitate every gesture. His teasing relaxed everyone including Ann.

Usually Calvin conducted from off stage, but the comic opera *What Price Confidence*, required four singers and a visible piano.

So for this one, the cast put him into costume and he directed out front where the audience loved him.

Everywhere they sang WOT received thunderous applause. At the Fairbanks Festival of the Arts the cast expected to perform with the local orchestra. Calvin flew ahead to rehearse, but the conductor, not trusting a stranger with his musicians, decided to play with them. Still, Calvin's eyes teared because in spite of brief rehearsals the orchestra responded to his every cue.

Arriving in Kivalina was a thrill. In this tiny village about one hundred miles north of the Arctic Circle, temperatures may drop to forty degrees below zero. Yet the entire population turned out to greet them. Eskimo children shyly waved crayoned signs of welcome. That night a few youngsters dressed as angels sang the lullaby they had learned in English just for the event. Opera was a new experience for these whalers, fishermen and hunters, and they wanted more.

A few days later, flying into Sitka proved to be difficult. The small plane carried only fifteen passengers, so the troupe arrived with neither scenery or costumes. Except for the maid, the cast performed in street clothes. Someone borrowed a waitress's apron from a nearby restaurant for that role, but lack of props and costumes did not matter. The audience loved the performance.

Bethel, in the far west tundra region where permafrost covers the land, was as far away as the troupe could go. Since there were no hotels, here the cast slept in private homes built on stilts above the ground.

Months before WOT was expected, Bethel's community had saved thousands of dollars to buy a Yamaha, their first community grand piano. The piano, the piano tuner and the singers all arrived on the same plane, and that afternoon several townspeople practiced duets, testing the sound of their new purchase.

Before the show began, an interpreter translated the opera into the Yukek Eskimo language. Afterwards, the villagers gave a huge feast of mussels, saffron-seasoned rice, chicken and peppers, which had been ordered weeks ahead from Anchorage. Throughout the night, with only one hour of darkness, everyone sang and joined in bold Greek dancing. After the singers left, the piano tuner stayed behind and tuned every upright piano in town.

Wherever WOT performed, critics said, "The casts were convincing, well played...great fun . . . ." and that Calvin "played with acumen (insight) and accuracy." Calvin toured with Western Opera Theater for three years before moving on.

- XII -
Glyndebourne, England

In 1974, Calvin was invited to join the prestigious Glyndebourne Opera Company in England, about which he told his friends, "One comes for more than the music. Glyndebourne is an experience!"

Glyndebourne's history is unique. Long before Calvin was born, its first concerts were informal. John Christie, owner of the estate and a bachelor, simply invited his friends, staff and tenants to listen to extracts from operas and sing in his spacious vaulted ceiling Elizabethan-style organ room. Christie himself sang a few roles, and although those were happy evenings, he felt unfulfilled.

When Christie married young soprano Audrey Mildmay, he decided to stage complete operas. So he designed a three hundred seat theater with a stage of considerable depth and had it constructed next to his manor house. As a visionary he also introduced some of the most advanced lighting equipment which his theater crew used.

On opening night, May 28, 1934, John Christie entertained fifty-five guests at a formal dinner. They dined after strolling through his gardens, then enjoyed Mozart's opera *Le Nozze di Figaro*. Several critics had resented the fifty-mile trip from London in tuxedos, but by the end of the evening they were raving about their Glyndebourne adventure.

Over the next thirty-four years Christie broadened the repertoire, extended the season and enlarged the wood-paneled theater to 800 seats. In 1961 his company gave the first opera at the Promendade Concerts in London's historic Royal Albert Hall. Six years later he sent the newly-formed Touring Opera through the English countryside. This custom which continues today gives young singers an opportunity to sing major roles in the smaller villages.

George Christie assumed the general directorship in 1958, four years before his father died. By the time Calvin arrived at Glyndebourne, opera tickets had become scarce, obtainable only through subscription. Today the list contains more than four thousand names of people who, hoping to become members of the Glyndebourne Festival Society wait for cancellations to this "hot ticket" event.

Glyndebourne singers come from many countries. Few are established stars. Like Calvin, they are usually talented and young.

It was Glyndebourne's music director, Sir John Pritchard, who invited Calvin to England in 1972. He had seen him conduct at the San Francisco Opera House, and told Christie, "Snap him up." George Christie later said, "Calvin was the only person among the *repetiteurs*, (staff members who assist musicians in their preparations to perform) who came with the score under his belt. Playing was almost as easy for him as doing a two-finger exercise. He had done his homework."

Calvin knew he was a curiosity. At twenty-four he was Glyndebourne's youngest member of the staff, its first American and the first black. In interviews he said, "I was the *colored* conductor, which upset me for months. But I realized they didn't mean any harm. They took me for a novelty." Still, for a joke and the better for Calvin to be seen, George Christie once had the inside of the prompter's box given a white background.

Calvin arrived in the spring with the cast and some of their families. No one came for the money. There were few days off and the pay was modest. But away from city noises they rehearsed undisturbed.

Calvin slipped smoothly into the Glyndebourne routine because he was used to being wherever he was needed. Music discussion started at breakfast and lasted until the 10:25 warning bell rang. Five minutes later Calvin and the cast met in the cold theater, where dust sheets covered all but the first two rows of seats.

For the next several weeks the director, conductor, and singers analyzed the opera scene by scene, exploring what singers wanted to do and how they felt in their roles. They discussed every gesture and every move. Over the weeks they assumed the characters they played on stage.

Working six hours a day, six days a week, they became a close-knit ensemble. Some singers found rehearsals difficult, but not Calvin. He repeated scenes as long as necessary until everyone was satisfied. John Christie had established rules which are still followed today. They presented operas in the Glyndebourne tradition—"the best that could be done anywhere."

Calvin loved everything about Glyndebourne—the green fields and grazing sheep, the apple orchards and flowering gardens, even the English misty weather, and especially the musty smell of the theater. Best of all, he loved his co-workers and delighted in breaking through their formal English manners.

On occasion, he sped through the Christie mansion, winding up all the clocks and giving each one a special name. Sometimes, in the middle of a solemn rehearsal, he started the Christie family game, "Touch You Last." Tagging someone on the sleeve, he raced through the theater and around a corner, chased by an adult or one of the four Christie children.

Calvin found a mischief-making friend in Richard Bradshaw. Once, on a free day, the pair boarded a boat to Paris where they rented a car. With Richard at the wheel and Calvin standing upright, they drove round and round the Arc de Triomphe shouting with joy. They missed the last boat home and did not sleep for three nights, but they had seen Paris! And Paris had seen them.

Excitement mounted when the London Philharmonic arrived. Relatives and friends of the cast and staff were invited to see the final rehearsals before opening night.

Glyndebourne always timed their fast-paced shows to train schedules. Patrons arrived from London and the South Coast around 4 p.m. Buses carried them from the station to the elegant estate and back to the station later in the evening. Tuxedoed gentlemen and formally clad ladies generally brought elaborate picnic baskets laden with silver, wine and gourmet food to be eaten during the seventy-five minute intermission on grassy carpet-like lawns.

Bradshaw said, "We pulled pranks whenever things started to get dull. It was the fashion for people to leave their picnics on the lawn to reserve their supper spot. While they were in the theater, Calvin and I would go 'round swapping the contents. The person with the (expensive) Fortnum and Mason delicacies would later open his hamper and find supermarket wine and pate. It all got sorted out, of course, and it made amusing conversation. Calvin and I would watch from behind the hedges doubled up with laughter."

In Calvin's second year at Glyndebourne, George Christie appointed him conductor for Glyndebourne's Touring Opera productions of, Mozart's *Cosí fan tutte* and *Don Giovanni*. Reviews varied, one critic thinking Calvin "did not always draw the finely Mozartian textures one expects." Another said Calvin's conducting was "one of the greatest pleasures . . . . He had command over his players and the music danced along. The London Philharmonic played with fizzing energy and needlepoint delicacy."

In 1975, besides appearing as conductor with the Touring Company, Calvin guest-conducted with the Scottish National Orchestra and the Halle Orchestra of Manchester, and in 1976 conducted the first performance of that season's production of *Le Nozze di Figaro*.

Allan Ulrich wrote: "The smile on Calvin's face that afternoon made the mellow English sunlight pale by comparison." Once again critics wrote differing reviews. One felt "the overture was done at a spanking pace . . . the energy often turned into a scramble." Another said Calvin got "delicate, detailed playing out of the orchestra."

A year later, however, George Christie was not satisfied. Calvin had overscheduled himself. He worked in England from May 9 through August 7, 1977. Then he conducted two concerts in the Los Angeles Hollywood Bowl and immediately returned to rehearse *Don Giovanni* at Glyndebourne. He flew back to America for another performance with the Los Angeles Philharmonic, where supported by a grant from the Rockefeller Foundation, he and the orchestra recorded the music for New World Records. A day later he was back in England conducting further rehearsals of *Don Giovanni* for the Touring Opera. Calvin himself called the summer "a killer" and August his "yo-yo month."

The Christies worried because Calvin did not conduct well. They felt he was not concentrating. Had they pushed him too fast? Sadly, they decided this would be his last season.

The dismissal hurt Calvin because he loved Glyndebourne and would have stayed forever, but the Christies gave him no choice. Nonetheless, he stayed in touch in his flamboyant style, with infrequent, expensive phone calls. The Christies considered Calvin "family" and missed him. They followed his successes with pleasure.

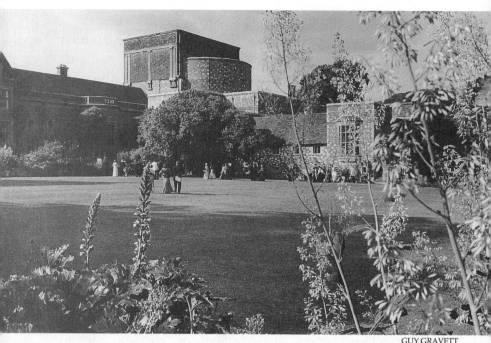

GUY GRAVETT

Glyndebourne's Organ Room and Opera House seen from the garden.

Music lovers picnic during intermission on the Glyndebourne grounds.

PHOTO COURTESY BRITISH TOURIST AUTHORITY.

- XIII -
Los Angeles

After three years with San Francisco Opera, Calvin decided he had to leave "home" to explore music possibilities elsewhere. Adler argued but Calvin insisted. Though Calvin knew he had upset his mentor, he entered a special competition and won an Exxon corporation fellowship.

Ernest Fleischmann, executive director of the Los Angeles Philharmonic, hired him as assistant to maestro Zubin Mehta. When Calvin moved from the Bay Area, he left behind thousands of saddened music lovers.

The *Chronicle* music critic, Robert Commanday, reasoned publicly that Sejii Ozawa, conductor of the San Francisco Symphony, should have chosen a qualified Californian rather than his new Swiss assistant. "Why not encourage local artists? Calvin Simmons is a superior musician who will be lost in Los Angeles," he predicted.

True, Calvin had joined a colossal organization whose orchestra performed in a vast metropolis. But he adapted well. His duties were similar to those performed for Mr. Adler. He coached guest artists and the chorus. He learned new scores and understudied conductors. "I waited for a conductor to cancel on short notice, but no one ever did," he said.

Life in Los Angeles was different from up North. Yet wherever Calvin worked, he radiated good humor. Whether at concerts given on gymnasium basketball courts, or in an auditorium, he first joked, then zapped the audience with music. When someone asked how he did it, he said modestly, "I try to play as fast as possible and I talk a lot."

He told one reporter, "I'm having a great time. I actually conduct about thirty performances a season—lots of kids' concerts and regular grown up programs which we take to Santa Barbara, Pasadena, Irvine, Palm Springs—all those little pin dots on the map."

He added, "You know...this orchestra must play more concerts than any other in the world . . . The morale is high . . . Ernest Fleischmann . . .he's dynamite. If there's any kind of personnel crisis, it's thrashed out immediately and solved."

Actually, Calvin did not entirely approve of Zubin Mehta's conducting. He rarely commented publicly but once he said, "I respect (Mehta) very much for what he does . . . but I disagree with him."

Mehta also had misgivings. He had not expected such a dynamic assistant. He said, "By the time Calvin came here, he had more than passed an assistant's role. He had a lot to say about music himself," so Mehta left him on his own, watching him only at a few high school and runout concerts. For the most part, it was Ernest Fleischmann who supervised Calvin's performances.

Calvin's Exxon grant divided his $20,000 a year salary between two positions—the Los Angeles Philharmonic and a directorship with the Los Angeles Young Musicians' Foundation Debut Orchestra. In this second assignment, he was in charge. He selected his staff, planned the programs and rehearsed the orchestra on Saturdays. This orchestra gave five concerts each season, and because these musicians could join at nineteen but had to leave at age twenty-five, Calvin had to hold auditions annually.

At the start the players were undisciplined and Calvin did not

respect their attitudes. He had to drive a long distance to rehearsals. Of Stravinsky's *The Rake's Progress* he said, "I didn't mind the
drive . . . Nobody showed up. Wow, that [orchestra] needs
organization. They have to get it together."

He was particularly angry when the Debut Orchestra and the
University of Southern California presented Purcell's two hundred year-old opera *Dido and Aeneas*—an opera that deals with
witches, sailors, Carthage and kings and queens. Calling the
performance a fiasco, he said, "That was a scandal . . . We just
barely got it on stage; it wasn't ready."

Eventually the musicians shaped up into a fine ensemble and
one critic called the group "decidedly mature." Bassoonist Rufus
Olivier remembers that the day he returned from an audition
with the San Francisco Symphony, Calvin stopped the rehearsal
to say, "By the way, I want to congratulate Rufus for winning
that gig." Playing in a major orchestra was everyone's goal so,
happy for Rufus, his peers applauded wildly.

Martin Bernheimer, critic for the *Los Angeles Times*, champi-
oned Calvin's talent from the beginning. After the Debut Orchestra played Beethoven's *Symphony #2*, he wrote: "The twenty-five-
year-old directed . . . with natural ease, a relaxed economy of
gestures and a reassuring amount of eye contact. He paced
movements in keeping with tradition and displayed a sharp ear
of airy balance."

Calvin loved his work but he missed the Bay Area and his
friends. One time he flew north for a small dinner party to
celebrate a friend's good fortune. During the evening he played
piano, did impromptu imitations and helped the hostess wash
dishes. Then he stretched out and dozed before flying south
again.

Calvin talked to strangers everywhere he went; that's how he
met doctor-reporter Tom Godfrey. They were browsing in a Los
Angeles music store. Godfrey, who had seen Calvin conduct,

recognized him and wanted to write his story. After several meetings Calvin became a special visitor to Kathy and Tom Godfrey's home.

Frequently he arrived with mysterious records to challenge Tom's musical knowledge, and Tom tried several musical quizzes on him. Keeping each other musically alert they also shared favorite old movies, such as *Bride of Frankenstein* and *Citizen Kane*.

Calvin especially loved the Godfrey's son Bryan. He referred to Bryan as "Little Calvin" until Kathy became pregnant again. Once he took Kathy's hand in his, patted her extended figure and asked, "Little Calvin?" He guessed right because the Godfreys named their second son after him.

As though conducting two orchestras wasn't enough, Calvin also applied for the directorship of the notable Ojai Festival. "We can't match your usual fee," a committee member said.

"Let's not discuss money. Let's not make that a problem," was Calvin's response. Once the money issue was dismissed, he was hired. Calvin selected his musicians from those he worked with in the Los Angeles Philharmonic, and also planned the programs. The concerts wowed the audiences and his reputation grew.

When Calvin made a guest appearance on the Johnny Carson "Tonight Show," Carson opened the conversation with, "I hear you're going to play a number—something ethnic no doubt."

Without a word, Calvin flipped his coat tails over the piano bench and began to play and sing, "Roamin' In the Gloamin'" with a strong Scottish burr. When he finished, sweetly he said, "Something ethnic." In spite of his cool attitude, Carson invited him back for a second show but Calvin refused.

In July 1975, when Calvin conducted an all-American program in the Hollywood Bowl, he took an amazing giant step forward. The program included "jazzy spirituals" and closed with rousing Sousa marches and spectacular fireworks, and everyone cheered.

Two summers later, on August 9, 1977, during that difficult summer of Glyndebourne commutes, Calvin conducted at the Bowl again. Chirping crickets and overhead planes did not prevent him from wooing the audience of more than ten thousand.

Of that evening Martin Bernheimer wrote: "Tuesday was a good night to be at the Hollywood Bowl. Calvin Simmons . . . took to the podium...and reminded us that he is a musician of rare individuality and authority . . . The orchestra played better than anyone has a right to expect under minimal rehearsal conditions in our gargantuan amphitheater."

Calvin began the Weber *Euryanthe* overture slowly. "He stressed old-school majesty...always allowing for the tired masterpiece to build... It was as sensible as it was mellow and stylish," Bernheimer wrote.

That same evening Calvin conducted Henry Gilbert's *Dance In Place Congo*, one of the numbers on the New World recording that was released months later. (This record is now available as a New World CD—NW 228.)*

Never one to remain idle, beside those dizzying trips between Los Angeles and England, Calvin guest-conducted with the Houston, Atlanta and American symphonies and the New York Philharmonic. Life was exhilarating, exhausting, and sometimes embarrassing.

One night after conducting the Atlanta Symphony, Calvin arrived at a reception in the home of a local hostess, still in his tuxedo. The hostess approached and asked, "Why now how do you do? What are you all doing here?" Responding to her perhaps mistaken belief that he was a hired waiter, Calvin flashed his grin and mimicked back in a flawless Southern accent, "Why

---

*Calvin cut a second record for Blue Notes, with the jazz vocalist, Carmen McRae, which is no longer available.

how do you do? I conducted the concert."

In 1976 Zubin Mehta announced his resignation from the Los Angeles Philharmonic, and people wondered whether Calvin wanted the directorship. "Me? . . . It would be a great mistake. It would be too soon, too early."

Mehta had become a full-fledged conductor at twenty-six, but Calvin reminded everyone that the orchestra had recently grown from minor to major status. "I'm not sure I'm ready for a job like that. There are other orchestras in this country that might be nice to build onto . . . ripe for upgrading," he said.

Nonetheless at twenty-seven, with his Glyndebourne and Philharmonic contracts coming to a close, Calvin was on the threshold of one more major change. Anything could happen.

Goodbyes to his Los Angeles friends were painful. Tears flowed with the champagne at a grand party. Still, as usual, Calvin kept in touch with friends by phone. Once he rang up Ernest Fleischmann just to say, "Hey Ernesto, I've just finished a week of looking over Dvořák's *4th Symphony* and I have absolutely fallen in love with it."

Calvin was looking forward to quiet hours for studying scores, but that was not to be. In January 1978, he directed *Hansel and Gretel* at the Metropolitan Opera House in New York. The Metropolitan audience applauded long after the curtain fell. Afterwards, Calvin took the opera on the road—to Buffalo, Philadelphia, Chicago and Washington, D.C. Although he had conducted it before he said, "I know my Metropolitan debut was a very important undertaking. But I get a cold back about such things . . . I still have a lot to learn . . ." After the tour, Calvin signed a contract to conduct a concert series in Los Angeles. This constant activity led one reviewer to call Calvin, "the young man of the hour, a conductor worth watching."

- XIV -
Coming Home

Calvin's Metropolitan Opera performance of *Hansel and Gretel* reached millions of people via a Texaco sponsored radio broadcast, and the Eastern U.S.A. tour that followed introduced him to thousands more. He then came home just when the Oakland Symphony was searching for a new conductor. This Symphony operated with a slim budget and paid its musicians only $6,000 a year in 1978, but it had a solid reputation.

The Oakland Symphony had an unusual beginning. After the City school board bought a boxcar of instruments for $10,000 a few amateur musicians joined together to make music at a local YMCA. Two years later, forty players presented a program of light classics in the lobby of a downtown office building.

Dr. Orley See, a Berkeley violin teacher, took charge in 1932, and the group named themselves the Oakland Symphony Orchestra. After Dr. See suddenly died, UC Symphony conductor Piero Bellugi became director until Gerhard Samuel took over in 1959. Under his leadership the Symphony's stature advanced. He added more youth concerts and as the budget increased, he introduced lesser known contemporaries including Arthur Berger, and Jacob Leteiner. He also invited more glamorous international soloists, Claudio Arrau, Isaac Stern, Artur Rubinstein and Van Cliburn to perform.

In 1961 the Symphony presented the West Coast premiere of Leonard Bernstein's *Chichester Psalms* to a sold-out audience.

Bernstein spent the better part of a year composing these complex psalms. A chorus and a boy alto heightened the score, which was sung in Hebrew. The music ranged from "suppressed jazz" to hauntingly slow movements and from meditative to modern dissonances. The televised concert brought national recognition, and in 1965 the Rockefeller Foundation awarded the orchestra a grant for its innovative programs.

Samuel was succeeded by Harold Farberman, who started free summer programs in the park and significant In-School Discovery concerts for young people.

In 1972 the City of Oakland bought the Paramount Theatre and remodeled the old movie house into a splendid concert hall. Its Art Deco interior was completely restored with its bronze-colored curtain, floral mohair-covered seats, sculptured ceiling grillwork and lighted, gilded gold-carved murals. This landmark building became the Symphony's permanent home.

Six years later when the Orchestra was seeking a new conductor, Calvin's name popped up. He was young, talented and his career spanned an ocean. Many hoped he would attract the city's large African American community to concerts. The hand-picked committee of civic leaders interviewed sixty candidates. Six, including Calvin, were invited as guest conductors during the 1978-1979 season.

Calvin knew he would be rehearsing musicians twice his age. Some had watched him grow up. Yet before their work sessions ended, several players asked the committee, "What are you waiting for? You've found your new director."

Eight days before Calvin's scheduled concert, the guest piano soloist fell ill and Deno Gianopoulous, a University of California music professor, stepped in. He and Calvin presented a terrific program. "Something wonderful happened at the Paramount Theatre... Shortly into the first movement of Dvořák's *8th Symphony* the coughing ceased [because]...the musicians, like the conductor, were playing by heart," one reviewer wrote.

Calvin followed this concert with two sellout nights at the outdoor Concord Pavilion, where he presented *Music From Outer Space*. With the first sounds, a brilliant single laser light beamed down at the foot of Mt. Diablo and shone for miles around. The light, centered at Calvin's feet, moved slowly over six thousand people who listened to the orchestra play popular themes from "Star Trek", *The Fury*, *Close Encounters of the Third Kind* and *Star Wars*.

Reviewers called the performance "inspiring, intelligent, instinctive, keenly sensitive . . . lyrical and musical to the core." Paul Hertelendy, then of the *Oakland Tribune* said, Calvin "cued perfectly, played the orchestra like a royal instrument, like a born conductor." After the final concert on April 29th, the crowd broke into a frenzy of prolonged cheers.

Later that night, the musicians and Calvin celebrated his twenty-eighth birthday at the Metropolitan Yacht Club. Standing before a huge cake, like an overgrown schoolboy, Calvin widened his eyes and chewed his nails. "Speech, speech!" everyone shouted. Facing his parents, Calvin blurted out to his friends, "I would be older if they had started sooner."

Then several musicians, playing a trumpet, a cello, a contrabassoon and a flute, serenaded Calvin with snippets from pieces he had recently conducted—Dvořák, Holst, Beethoven and John Williams, which principal percussionist Jerome Neff had skillfully arranged that morning.

Shortly after the party, rumors flew. Calvin was an obvious favorite. In July, after he conducted Mozart's *Requiem* at Berkeley's Zellerbach Hall, the committee announced that he was their unanimous choice, at a starting salary of $40,000 a year.

The *Chronicle* music critic Robert Commanday wrote "He's bright and he doesn't pose or pretend. People will pull for him." Calvin modestly told reporters, "Nobody at twenty-eight knows all he's supposed to know. I hope I will continue to grow and improve. I feel . . . I'm becoming something complete."

Suddenly Calvin was big news. He went into the community, attending fifty-five "Meet the Conductor" parties in churches and private homes. Everyone wanted to know who his favorite composers were, his favorite operas and how he felt about modern music.

"At this stage in my career . . . I have to grab onto everything . . . not say, 'Humph. I'm not going to do this or that.'" He recalled that Rossini's opera, *Barber of Seville*, and Bizet's *Carmen* "had induced outrage or riots and were considered disasters when they premiered." Modern music? He had heard Benjamin Britten's music while in the Boys Chorus. "Everything that man wrote has something to say to me," he said.

Calvin told Fred Tulan, a designer of organs for the Metropolitan Opera, the Philadelphia Orchestra and the San Francisco Symphony, that he wanted to introduce more music by young composers, and that he knew he had not yet learned as much as he would.

When a reporter asked, "Calvin, when do you expect to marry?" he replied, "I am already married."

"I didn't know that. When did it happen?"

"I married when I was six. I'm married to music and when I find someone I love deeply, I'll marry in the conventional way."

There were some people who suggested that Calvin won the post because of his color. "I had to be qualified . . . I don't see colors. I see black and white all right, but it's only in the score." Repeatedly he emphasized, "I can only think of myself as a musician. If there's going to be an impact, it's going to be through the music I make."

But Calvin *was* a trailblazer. Few African Americans play in major orchestras, and even today black conductors are few and far between.

Even though Dean Dixon founded the New York City (radio) chamber orchestra, he mostly worked abroad. Calvin knew Dixon's story well. He once said, "Years ago Dean Dixon was having the worst time . . . he went away to Germany very bitter."

Born in 1915, in New York City, the son of West Indian immigrants, Dean Dixon studied violin before he was four, and in DeWitt Clinton High School organized an amateur seventy piece orchestra. After graduating Juilliard (1936) and earning a masters from Columbia (1937) he became the first African American to conduct the New York Philharmonic and the NBC (radio) Symphony. But he chose to live where he was valued for his talent.

He became music director of Sweden's Goteberg Symphony, the Hessischer Rundfund symphony in Germany and Australia's Sydney Symphony Orchestra.

Twenty years later when he returned to the United States, he conducted the New York Philharmonic in Central Park before an enthusiastic crowd of 75,000 people. The Schlitz Brewing Company then sponsored a successful eight-city tour. But, Dixon never held a full conductorship in his own country.

Henry Lewis became "the first African American of a standard American Symphony when he was appointed music director of the New Jersey Symphony Orchestra in 1968."

There is also James DePriest, a nephew of Marian Anderson, who served as assistant conductor of the New York Philharmonic, held the post of associate conductor of the National Symphony of Washington and was music director of the Quebec and Oregon Symphonies.

Usually however, when people consider serious black musicians they think of the famous singers—Marian Anderson, Paul Robeson, Leontyne Price and Jessye Norman. And although Henry Lewis was the first African American conductor at the Metropolitan Opera, *The New York Times* wrote, "Simmons is the only black music director of a major symphony in the United States." Actually, Calvin became the first black conductor of a major orchestra *west* of the Mississippi and Calvin knew he was a history-maker.

When someone asked him how many black musicians were in Oakland's orchestra, Calvin said, "I'm it!" Perhaps because he was IT, the black community came out and supported him. When they lined up after concerts to shake his hand, he jokingly said, "They're all my relatives. Really!"

Calvin knew older more experienced conductors led symphonies better than he did, that he "was a baby, as conductors go." He said, "I have to start and let the critics howl. I don't mind making mistakes if I learn from them . . . I'm the one who has to stand up and conduct. If I don't believe in a work, I'm certainly not going to convince the public."

But convince the public he did. The Symphony was in good shape, "on a level wonderful to grow from," he said. "Some people think I'm going to revolutionize music in Oakland in three months. It doesn't happen overnight."

Nevertheless, he brought rapid changes. He was the Symphony's best salesman. Wherever he talked—on radio, before audiences, in private homes—his intense love for music spoke for him. Contributions increased and subscriptions rose by twenty percent. The William and Flora Hewlett Foundation provided a fellowship for minority musicians to play in the orchestra.

Calvin believed "Music must not be allowed to stand still," so he began fall concert season preparations months ahead. "Nobody wants all Mozart and Brahms...an orchestra must be able to deal with layers of sound." He included contemporary music with classics, and under his leadership the orchestra flourished. "Under Calvin the music seemed to flow," piccolo player Eugene Kushner said.

Calvin paced his musicians with both love and discipline. If rehearsals became fussy or furious, he sometimes referred to old movies to lighten the mood. One musician recalls him saying, "Listen, I want this to sound a little more like Lana Turner looks in the moonlight."

Everyone came to rehearsals in casual clothes, Calvin preferring turtlenecks or open-collared shirts and soft sweaters. He also occasionally wore steel rimmed glasses, which most fans did not see in public.

After he joined the Oakland Symphony, Calvin laid his baton aside. He signaled instead with his eyes, a facial expression or by waving his thin arms and hands. "Who needs a stick? You think people see that itsy bitsy little white line? The baton is a crutch that prevents music from coming straight through me," he said. He believed his players listened more carefully to one another when the baton was out of the way, and he felt audiences could always watch his hands. (The famous Leopold Stokowski had many years before fascinated the public by conducting the Walt Disney movie *Fantasia* with batonless hands.) Verez Olshausen said, "His hands were humming birds expressing the dartings of his mind [and] his senses."

Calvin memorized complete scores but kept the music on his stand for reference. With feet planted firmly, he leaned forward, sometimes grabbing a fistful of air to exaggerate a passage. At times he began a piece with an audible, "Burrump, burrump," or a downbeat. Or he sang along, "Umpbub, pop-bub-bub. Good!"

Calvin believed that he and the orchestra were a team. He never criticized musicians in public. One look from him and they knew what he wanted. If he lectured on a point, he spoke to an entire section, not to an individual. He might say, "That needs a lot of work" or "This is very sloppy." One time he thundered at the whole orchestra, "How many of you practice scales every day? You must play scales. SCALES! Why Rudi Serkin, no matter how many times he has played a concerto, goes into his barn every morning and practices scales for an hour."

Basic things like poor lighting, unnecessary noise and physical backstage problems disturbed him. Once, when someone blundered, he asked, "What is this, Mickey Mouse?"

Calvin always supported the musicians. The day they met in the freezing, unoccupied Oakland Technical High School, he first called the management to complain, then announced, "We can't rehearse here. Go home. Everyone is getting paid." His concern for the musicians was undisguised. Calvin excited the public, and the community responded as never before. Lovingly, they welcomed their young conductor back to the Bay Area.

- XV -
Opening Night

On October 16, 1979, the Paramount Theatre lit the downtown streets of Oakland, California. Buses, autos, sleek limousines and trains brought three thousand people into the city for a gala evening.

People came from San Francisco, San Mateo, Marin County and nearby towns. Oakland's mayor and council members, music lovers and first-time concertgoers, the rich and not so rich, the young, middle-aged and older citizens dressed in their best mingled with celebrities.

Crowds three feet deep filled the theater lobby, everyone surging forward to glimpse wall mounted photographs of Calvin Simmons, their home-grown hero. Many wondered whether this energetic twenty-nine year-old would live up to his advance publicity: "SYMPHONY—PLUS SIMMONS—SENSATION-AL!"

Promptly at 8 p.m. trumpeters sounded a brassy ceremonial fanfare from the broad theater staircase, and people hurried to their seats. The Oakland Symphony's forty-sixth season was about to open. Calvin's parents and his life-time friends Madi Bacon, Peggy Fahrner, William Duncan Allen, Louise and Frank McTernan sat in the fourth row, where Calvin could see them when he bowed.

On stage, concertmaster Nathan Rubin signaled the oboist to sound an "A," and the musicians tuned their instruments.

Kurt Herbert Adler, director of the San Francisco Opera and Calvin's first boss, was almost late. Rushing backstage he met Calvin coming from his dressing room and gave him a firm pat on the shoulder. Calvin flashed him a broad grin. His slim body clothed in a well-tailored tailcoat, tall and graceful, Calvin strode toward the curtain and paused. Out of backstage darkness a stagehand called, "Are you ready?"

"Of course I'm ready," Calvin said. A second voice said, "Good luck," and Calvin marched confidently out of the wings onto the stage. He shook hands with the concertmaster and turned as the audience broke into thunderous applause and affectionate shouts. Then he raised three fingers, signaled the downbeat, and Mozart's *Magic Flute* overture filled the theater.

The hushed audience listened, intent and satisfied. In the second number, he led not only the orchestra but the large Symphony chorus and four soloists through Mozart's "Thamos, King of Egypt." During Mussorgsky's *Pictures at an Exhibition*, Calvin's body swayed gently with the music, "putting a little soul into it," someone said.

At the final chord the audience rose for a standing ovation. Calvin applauded his musicians until they too, were on their feet. Only then did he turn around to bow and accept the applause with them.

His friend, Kori Lockhart, was waiting in his dressing room. As they embraced, he asked, "How do you think it went?"

If he did not know, the public quickly showed him. Enthusiastic fans lined the theater aisles, waiting patiently to congratulate and compliment him. Afterwards, five hundred people celebrated with him at a champagne party in the Kaiser Center.

Newspaper reviews were mixed. One critic thought the voices of the soloists and chorus were "brilliant as silver." Another said Calvin "conducted almost too carefully, but perhaps that's well for starters . . . During *Pictures at an Exhibition* he walked on eggs." But he added, "Calvin is a rare and special person, honest with himself, honest with his players."

Ernest Fleischmann said, "Calvin thinks music. He dreams music and he has a lot of charisma." And, Blake Samson of the *Contra Costa Times* raved. "Greatness is given to but a few. The city that has a man like Calvin Simmons and an orchestra like the Oakland Symphony has wealth beyond any city treasure chest!"

*(Above) Calvin posed
in front of the
Curtis Institute
during his
student days.*

*(At right) Calvin
and his friend "Frenchie"
hug during a visit
home from college.*

Counselor Calvin asks "Whose sweater is this?"

DICK MEYER

(Below) Philip Kelsey and Calvin rehearsed with choristers for a production of "All the King's Men."

Alongside the volleyball court, Calvin teaches the younger boys music theory at SFBC Camp.

DICK MEYE

LOUISE MCTERNAN

Calvin liked to study scores at the home of
Frank and Louise McTernan.

(Right) Calvin stands alongside his shiny, new BMW.

(Below) Crowds listened to Calvin conduct The Threepenny Opera *on San Francisco street corners.*

(Above)Beverly Sills smiles through her prima donna skit with Calvin during an annual Fol de Rol *fundraiser.*

(Below) Beverly Sills studies the score of Juana, La Loca *with composer Gian Carlo Menotti.*

(Above) Calvin enjoys a social event with his mother, Mattie Pearl, and his friend and director of SFBC, Madi Bacon.
(Below) Henry Calvin Simmons shares a pleasurable evening with his son.

The Oakland Symphony performed concerts in the elegantly refurbished Oakland Paramount Theater.

Calvin hid in the curtain-folds of the San Francisco Opera House.

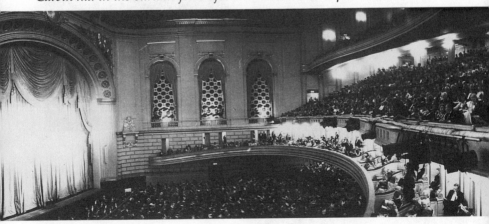

KEN HOWARD

Calvin's activities included . . .

ROBERT REITER

. . . lunch at Trader Vic's . . .
. . . pausing for a photo with a
young fan.

. . . blowing out candles on a
huge cake, Calvin celebrated his
28th birthday with the Oakland
Symphony musicians before he
became their conductor.

(Left) Calvin G., named for
Calvin, like him , is "gregarious,
bright, inquiring and
challenging."

BETTY JANE NEVIS

BETTY JANE NEVIS

BETTY JANE NEVIS

Calvin and the Stars

(Clockwise from top left) Calvin and Leontyne Price; Victor Borge and Calvin lock arms; with Yehudi Menuhin.

(Right) Calvin with his friend, pianist and music critic, William Duncan Allen.

(Below) Calvin called conductor Max Rudolf his most important teacher, "a walking encyclopedia."

(Left) The Cast from "An Orchestra Is A Team Too!" Calvin, Joe Namath, Ricky Schroeder and an unidentifed actor posed for publicity.

(Bottom) After hiking its trails, Calvin conducted Grofe's Grand Canyon Suite *to the Canyon itself.*

(Above) Calvin sometimes wore glasses during orchestra rehearsals.

(Below) Calvin and Jonathan Miller pause with a couple attending Cosí fan tutte in St. Louis.

- XVI -
Work and Play

Calvin, like Adler, wanted to bring music to as many people as possible. Audiences might choose to applaud or not, but he at least wanted them to hear music. He felt, "Hearing Beethoven should be as personal as listening to the Rolling Stones."

Calvin reached out for larger audiences by arranging for distribution of free tickets for students, seniors and disabled persons, and he took the orchestra on the road. They played in nearby Contra Costa County, Hayward, Castro Valley, Alameda, in Stockton, Davis and Santa Cruz, and as far away as Santa Barbara, and they became known as "the most traveled orchestra in the state."

Calvin believed children especially have a right to hear classics at an early age. Because he remembered his own childhood filled with music, he dropped into Oakland schools unannounced to talk with students and the students became fans.

Calvin's first concerts which were conventional, included an overture, a concerto and a symphony. Gradually he introduced some of the lesser known English composers—Benjamin Britten, Gustav Holst, Thea Musgrave and Sir Michael Tippett. Like Gerhard Samuel before him, he promoted local soloists, and he also invited superstars to perform, among them Itzhak Perlman, Leontyne Price and Yehudi Menuhin. Several who were guests with the Oakland Symphony—Richard Stoltzman, Jeffrey Kahane, Leona Mitchell and Paul Tobias—have since become stars.

Like most conductors, Calvin knew what he wanted to hear, so shortly after taking the directorship, he revived an eighteenth century custom. By rearranging the string section, placing first violinists to his left and second violinists on his right, he felt the audience would listen to a better blending of tones and the musicians would also become more aware of each other.

Where other conductors might tell stories or give lengthy explanations for what they wanted, Calvin could say one word—SPAIN—followed by a sharp up-down stroke, and the fiery passion and sunlight of Debussy's *Iberia* came forth.

During a particular cello passage in one rehearsal, Calvin started to sing, "I don't know," along with the music. In repeated phrases, a cellist joined him. Days later, while performing publicly, the cellist and Calvin exchanged sly grins, enjoying their private joke.

Critics praised performance after performance. When André Watts played Rachmaninoff's *Piano Concerto #2*, Calvin and the orchestra accompanied him sensitively like a shadow. Afterwards the *Sacramento Bee* wrote: "Watts with Calvin Simmons and the Oakland Symphony . . . 'perfect rapport.' At the end of the final movement—thunder indeed! The crashing chords were like a shout of 'Hallelujah!' The audience was on its feet cheering!"

Calvin accepted all praise. But because he knew there was more work to be done, he did not let compliments influence his musical judgment.

Pianist Peter Orth recalled his first rehearsal with Calvin. While he was practicing alone on stage, Calvin danced over and introduced himself. Laughing together, the informality made performing more comfortable.

Calvin chose soft-spoken Kent Nagano, as his assistant. At first Kent found Calvin's style irritating, because he liked to correct mistakes as they happened. Calvin preferred to emphasize the positive. It took time for Nagano to appreciate this approach. Nevertheless, Calvin used Nagano's talent well.

Nagano became Calvin's "roving ears," his scout who listened to how the orchestra's sound came to every corner of the Paramount Theater. He also screened and recommended new scores, rehearsed the musicians in Calvin's absence and stood ready to conduct if Calvin might fail to show up for a performance. But Calvin, who had waited for a similar opportunity to conduct the Los Angeles Philharmonic, was always there! He even appeared and conducted the night his car spun out of control and went up an embankment. After the concert he told Kent, "That was the closest you got to going on stage."

Although he did not give Kent an opportunity to conduct the Symphony, he applauded vigorously when Nagano conducted for the Oakland Ballet, and, he pushed him into directing the Oakland Youth Symphony Orchestra.

Though Calvin and Kent came from different backgrounds (Kent is Japanese-American) at times the two felt like brothers.

Kent was born into a close-knit family in Berkeley. His father was studying architecture, his mother music, until the family moved to Morro Bay to care for and work his grandfather's farm.

Like Calvin, Kent studied piano with his mother at age four, and music became a happy part of his home life. In high school he played a variety of instruments, including the koto, viola and clarinet. But unlike Calvin, he first studied law at Oxford, England, before at age twenty-one, music won out. Just a year younger than his boss, Kent worked well with Calvin.

Soon after Calvin returned to the Bay Area, he rented a house in the Berkeley Hills which became his hideaway high in the clouds. He filled his home with a mix of inherited furniture, some carefully chosen stereo equipment and a small grand piano. The walls were decorated with pictures of famous trains and the French ship, the *Normandie*.

Alone in his den late at night, Calvin liked to gaze at the stars or study scores. He was a soap opera fan and so often watched taped videos of "General Hospital." Cooking was not a high priority. Calvin ate well only because his mother and his friend Mary Maehl, who was the Symphony's publicity director, stocked his freezer with roasts and casseroles. Or, on the spur of the moment he dropped in for make-do dinners with Madi, Mary or Kori Lockhart.

Friends who visited came to mostly potluck parties. But Calvin did prepare one Thanksgiving dinner for his parents, Madi and another friend. That day he had to borrow flour for the gravy from his neighbors, Etta and Irwin Shapiro.

When he was at home, Calvin liked to telephone the Shapiros to tell them about a quail or rabbit that was in his yard at the moment. Sometimes he asked to borrow their dog for a walk in the hills. Whenever he traveled for concerts, they kept their eyes on his property, and he often returned with a gift for them.

Calvin worked hard, but he also liked to play. One day he enticed Kent into a hike through wet fields in nearby Tilden Park. Idling along, they suddenly spotted a herd of cattle racing toward them. Quick-footed and undignified, the two conductors ran through tall grasses and climbed a stone fence, with pounding hooves inches and seconds behind them.

Disciplined as Calvin's conducting habits were, his personal papers were a mess. When Peggy Fahrner's son, Bob, agreed to become his personal manager, Calvin wrote on his calendar, "Hallelujah! Bob Fahrner starts today!" Bob adapted easily and Calvin trusted him.

One day while Bob was checking accounts, Calvin swaggered across the living room wearing a wide-brimmed cowboy hat, then he disappeared. Minutes later, back sporting a fedora, he sang, danced, acted the comic and disappeared again. He returned once more to sing various roles from an opera he was preparing before going back to work. Antics like these helped him relax.

When he got the urge, Calvin drove to the Sierra to visit with Peggy Fahrner and Iris Mann in their home. There he sat on the deck listening to the chatter of squirrels and birds, or he walked along the empty roads, sniffing the sweet aroma of pine trees. Nature's "music" soothed him. When guests filled the house, he joined in the singing and game playing and felt almost as if he were back in camp.

Calvin loved new adventures. One friend introduced him to golf but he played a terrible game. Occasionally he flew east to Lake Placid, New York, for a visit with his longtime friend from early opera days, Richard Rodzinski. One vacation he hiked down the Grand Canyon trails. He scuffed the red earth on his new boots to make them look worn and wore with pride a ribbon that read, "I hiked Bright Angel Trail." Before leaving the Canyon, he stood on top of a bluff and sang and conducted Grofe's *Grand Canyon Suite* to the canyon itself!

During his second year with the Oakland Symphony, Calvin started a "Pops" series because he believed people would respond to all kinds of music. "If you convince three thousand people that what you've done is wonderful, you've done a pretty good job," he told a reporter.

That same season he introduced concerts to thousands of children and their parents. Calvin chose the music, and cartoonist Morrie Turner created a *Wee Pals* slide show. The *Wee Pals* characters rode space ships, explored jungles and became cowboys. Musical notes turned into a ball thrown at a dog, into pogo sticks, or golf clubs.

As his popularity grew, Calvin began to guest-conduct in opera houses and concert halls all over the country—in Philadelphia, New York, Detroit, Buffalo, Los Angeles, Atlanta, Kansas

City, and in Canada's Vancouver, Winnipeg and Toronto. The Oakland community did not mind. He was after all, *their* discovery!

On short notice, he once stepped in for the Russian conductor, Yuri Temirkanov, who had to cancel an engagement with the Minnesota Orchestra. Calvin changed the program to include the seldom-heard Schubert *Symphony #6*, instead of Rimsky-Korsakov's *Scheherazade*, and critics called his conducting "serious, intelligent, and adroit." A great triumph for him.

All performances, however, were not easy. When Gian Carlo Menotti wrote *Juana La Loca* for Beverly Sills' final operatic role, she in turn invited Calvin to be her conductor.

Problems arose from the beginning. *San Diego Tribune* reviewer Andrea Herman wrote that "the San Diego Opera production of *La Loca* was somewhat of a miracle." Known for lateness, Menotti delivered his final notes in the afternoon on the day of the performance. Four hours later the cast of fifty held its dress rehearsal of the third act.

Ms. Sills said, "Through it all, Calvin was funny . . . keeping us close like a family." Actually, having conducted Menotti's music before, he knew that the composer sketched characters loosely enough to give both the conductor and singers opportunity to interpret the music.

Juana La Loca tells the life of Juana, daughter of King Ferdinand and Queen Isabelle of Spain. As heir to the throne, she is accused by her father, her husband and her son of being mad and spends most of her life in prison. During the first act when Juana (Ms. Sills) understands her husband's nature, "she wept so naturally some audience members were moved [too]." Later, when a chorus member screamed unexpectedly after stepping on a backstage hot wire, Ms. Sills calmly waited for Calvin's cue and made the sudden cry offstage appear to be part of the plot.

In the final scene, she portrayed a wrinkled, now truly crazy queen. Ms. Sills got into her part so deeply, she had "to sit still three or four minutes in order to recover," before taking her bow.

Ms. Herman wrote that "Simmons led the orchestra with affectionate power . . . with few rehearsals [his] judgments . . . were purely instinctive. He coaxed spirit from the orchestra." She concluded by saying, Menotti's opera "ought to be a work of art never to be forgotten." In spite of delays and mishaps the opera was a great success.

Calvin did not think much about fame or money. For him, at least, that was not what conducting was about. "There has to be something else," he said. "A very high feeling that is passed on." He was not without ego, but Calvin felt he would not try to outdo other conductors. "I'm just incredibly happy doing what I'm doing."

His fame did somewhat surprise his father. One day while flying a United airliner, Mr. Simmons watched the man next to him open the airline magazine *Mainliner* to a full page photograph of Calvin. "A fine young man," the stranger said. Reaching into his wallet, Mr. Simmons pulled out a photo of Calvin, and smiling broadly, said, "That's my son!"

In 1981 Calvin joined Joe Namath and Ricky Schroeder in the CBS children's TV special, "An Orchestra Is a Team Too." Namath talked about conductors and coaches, and Calvin conducted the American Symphony through "The Dream of The Witches Sabbath" from Berlioz' *Fantastic Symphony*.

The TV film explored how similar football teams and orchestras are. While football coaches call field plays, a conductor signals musicians with his eyes, hands and body. Football players exercise before the game. Musicians limber up their fingers and practice breath control. When someone triumphs either on the field or in a concert hall, crowds cheer.

Calvin loved making this film. When there was a lull in the shooting, he read jokes from little cards he pulled from his wallet. The musicians appreciated his diligence and humor and nicknamed him, "Superleader, Calvin Simmons."

By the time the film appeared on TV, Calvin was back in San Francisco undertaking still one more major project. Maestro Kurt Adler had asked him to prepare to conduct the difficult, rarely seen, and politically suppressed opera, Shostakovich's *Lady Macbeth of Mtsensk* (also known as *Katerina Ismailova*).

- XVII -
Lady Macbeth of Mtsensk

A single clarinet's voice filled the San Francisco Opera House. Slowly, weepy tones of eerie violins grew into a frenzy of striking sounds. On September 19, 1981, the opera curtain rose onto a stark set of weather-beaten houses and bleak interiors alerting the audience that the violent tale of *Lady Macbeth of Mtsensk* was about to unfold.

Lady Macbeth of Mtsensk portrays every known emotion—love, sorrow, anger, terror, violence, intrigue and death. The plot tells about a merchant's wife, Katerina, who is a strong woman. She does not respect her dull, cowardly husband and will not permit her father-in-law to bully her. Lonely and bored, she falls in love with a forceful scoundrel who brings out the worst in her. Eventually, in seeking justice and revenge, Katerina kills three people and, on the way to exile in Siberia, kills her rival and herself.

Dmitri Shostakovich was twenty-six and courting his future wife, Nina Varza, when he composed this opera. He based his heroine on a character in a novel written in 1840. While Katerina seems villainous, the composer actually wanted people to sympathize with her because she was fighting against deceitful men. For Shostakovich, Katerina represented all Russian women who were seeking freedom in a male-dominated society.

The Russian audiences were shocked when the opera opened in 1932. The three-and-a-half hour tragedy played two hundred performances but the Russian leaders, who preferred folk tales with happy endings, disliked it. They thought the story was gruesome, the music too experimental and its dissonant, clashing notes made them uneasy.

After seeing just one act, dictator Joseph Stalin stormed from the theater calling the music "degenerate." He believed the opera accused the government of oppression and so suppressed it almost immediately. Shostakovich was labeled "an enemy of the people" and found himself in deep trouble. For a while he feared for his life. He felt hounded, like a "criminal...always under suspicion." (Yet a decade later he said writing the score was "the happiest... time of my music.")

In 1936, when Artur Rodzinski (conductor and father of Calvin's friend Richard) was doing a concert tour of Russia, he persuaded Shostakovich to let him bring the opera back to America. The Ministry of Culture gave Rodzinski permission to take the opera with him, but a border patrol mistaking the dots that plotted stage positions for Russian military secrets, seized the score. Rodzinski argued and managed to convince them to let him carry the treasured music home, and when the opera opened in New York, American audiences were stunned.

Shostakovich revised the opera in 1956 and renamed it *Katerina Ismailova*. Seven years later, when it was performed again in Russia, it was a success. The following year the San Francisco Opera presented *Katerina Ismailova* in English.

Lady Macbeth of Mtsensk fascinated Calvin. He knew how the opera was brought into this country, and he preferred the original score. Adler and he decided to mount the exact version that had angered Stalin. Calvin selected a cast of mostly American singers, and everyone learned Russian by rote.

Calvin lived, breathed, and totally immersed himself in the story. For months he studied the music and read everything he could find about the composer and the opera. He sat alone and just stared at the score for days. He turned his head into a "photo machine," repeatedly visualizing how the opera might be staged. He listened to tapes, sang arias himself and played passages on the piano. Even New Wave music of "The Police" and "Diva" suggested dramatic ideas. When he visited his friend Richard, he placed a photo of Artur Rodzinski on the piano for inspiration.

Calvin prepared for *Lady Macbeth of Mtsensk* along with the work he was doing during his regular concert season. He coached the orchestra and singers separately and ironed out rough spots with the concertmaster, Zaven Melikian. In turn, Melikian worked with the violinists. When the singers and orchestra finally met, every moment was electric. They rehearsed together only for ten hours.

Calvin worked well with everyone. Evelyn de la Rosa, who played the maid Aksinya, remembers his special kindness to her. They were working on her tricky role, and he appreciated that she came well prepared. "Let's hit it," he said, and Ms. de la Rosa had fun with her part.

Tall and willowy German soprano Anja Silja was a perfect Katerina. She used her face, her body and her voice to project a vital, intelligent woman. Her every gesture evoked sympathy. Whether she stood motionless on stage, took a sponge bath, or murdered those who had harmed her, Anja Silja's portrayal of Katerina held the audience entranced. She was so good, the cast thought of her as Katerina all the time.

Appearing early in the first act, Evelyn de la Rosa had to walk across the stage in front of boisterous mill workers. The men teased, chased and pinched her. She said, "They lifted me onto a scale as though I was a sack of flour, then twirled me around. All this went on while we were all singing a mile a minute." Shostakovich used the maid to show an example of how badly men treated women.

After singing in each performance, Evelyn de la Rosa ripped off her babushka (head kerchief) and costume, hurried into street clothes, and joined standees in the back of the theater. From off-stage she watched her colleagues perform, and before the opera ended she raced to change back into costume, and take her bows with the rest of the cast.

Opening night attracted music lovers and music critics from across the country and Europe. They came to see the Russian version of *Lady Macbeth of Mtsensk*, which had not been performed in the United States for forty-five years.

The orchestra played with such zealous conviction that during the more violent passages, Calvin's body quivered. Someone thought he looked like a Cossack bursting into dance. During two intermissions, not wanting to break the mood, the musicians played what Calvin called "circus music," while stagehands changed the scenery on a darkened stage. During one scene, although no one was singing, the audience spontaneously and without apparent reason broke into thunderous applause. Few people understood Russian but the music held them spellbound. After the first act the audience clapped, stomped their feet and exploded into cheers, shouting bravos for Calvin and Anja Silja. They whooped and shouted again when the final curtain came down. The season's least-likely-to-succeed opera had become the hit of the year!

Well-wishers crowded into his dressing room and Calvin pulled up his trouser legs. "For a Russian opera you wear red socks!" he said. With sandals in mind, Mary Maehl asked, "And what will you wear for a Greek opera?"

"No socks at all!" responded Calvin.

Nationwide, mentioning nearly everyone in the cast, reviewers raved about the new production. *The New York Times* said Calvin's music lit fires. *Time* magazine called the evening "an unqualified triumph, a musical treat at its blazing best! Most impressive was Calvin Simmons, 31. He threw himself into the music with single-minded intensity . . . fanning the opera's central fires to white hot incandescence."

Calvin summed up what everyone in the cast felt. "When we first did *Lady Macbeth of Mtsensk*, there was a feeling that it might not succeed. We did five performances and they were thronged. Some people came all five times!"

This opera became Calvin's brilliant and personal tribute to Kurt Herbert Adler, who was closing his final year as general director of the Opera Company.

Conducting batonless, Calvin let his face, his eyes and hand guide the musicians.

- XVIII -
The Whirlwind Year

The success of *Lady MacBeth of Mtsensk* raised Calvin's stature in the music world. In 1982, during the Symphony season he was invited to team with Jonathan Miller to do Mozart's two-act opera, *Cosí fan tutte* in St. Louis. Friends gave him a send-off birthday party and because he insisted on wearing every present, when the last gift was unwrapped, Calvin wore two hats, running trunks over pants, an Italian silk sweater and a Save-the-Whales-T-shirt. He was not looking forward to this trip, yet it would prove to be a highlight in his life.

The St. Louis Opera Festival, is like Glyndebourne, respected worldwide. Richard Gaddes, the company's founder and general director, each year presented operas in an intimate 950-seat theater. His singers were young and undiscovered, and many went on to fame. Caring as he did about his casts and directors, Gaddes gave them the freedom to develop productions in their own style.

Jonathan Miller and Calvin had met years before at Glyndebourne. Miller, a doctor-author-actor-director of theater and opera, has juggled his multiple careers well. Among his projects, he has directed Shakespearean plays for the BBC (British Broadcasting Company) and produced "The Body In Question," a medical TV series. Big art show biz did not interest Miller, but Mozart's world did. About director Gaddes he said, "I would go anywhere for this man."

"One privilege of doing works from the past is to be able to break bread with the dead," Miller told his cast. He and Calvin were a perfect match. "It was as though they both decided separately to demonstrate how a quality conductor-director partnership can work," someone commented.

Calvin and the cast met for the first time on a hot spring afternoon in a deserted school room. Singers Ashley Putnam and Patricia McCaffey had apprenticed together at the Santa Fe Opera. Tenor Jerry Hadley and baritone Thomas Hampson would share major roles with John Stephens and Ruth Golden. Calvin gave the downbeat, banged on the rinky-dink school piano and in spite of the heat, the singers sang out Mozart's lyric magic.

The group concentrated on the positive and were inspired by each other's creativity. Occasionally Miller prowled about to demonstrate how a character might behave, or said simply, "That's jolly good," or "Splendid." Calvin nodded in approval and kept the mood upbeat. To call for the cast to rest, he signaled by playing a fast piano chorus of a pop tune, "You Are My Sunshine." His humor helped Miller and everyone else to relax.

"Calvin understands that rehearsing has to be fun," Miller said. "If it isn't fun, it's absolutely awful." Both men felt rehearsals were serious work but they didn't exhaust themselves by worrying about them.

After rehearsals, the tall, skinny pair—Miller in seersucker and Calvin wearing a white suit and a Panama straw hat—spent time singing arias, going on shopping sprees, or roaming the city with the troupe. Evenings, they listened to jazz in cafes or jitterbugged at the Casa Loma ballroom.

Two days before opening night, Miller went into a gloomy tailspin. His job was almost over; the opera now "belonged to the singers." On the other hand, Calvin "was dying to be 'up there' doing it!" Opening night, June 3, 1982, was a smashing success.

The audience loved everything—the sets, the voices, the action. *The St. Louis Post-Dispatch* said that Calvin's music was "buoyant and rhythmic . . . Simmons is clearly an exceptional young musician." *The New York Times* critic wrote, "A more provocative and consistant '*Così*' you are not likely to come across in a lifetime of opera-going." And about Miller he said, "It remains to be proven whether he is or can become the best opera director in the world."

The cast was greeted with standing ovations after every performance. Calvin emerged from the pit and joined in the last bow. On the last night he cried, realizing this would be their final time together. Before leaving the stage, as the group clasped each other's hands, all were in tears.

A festive benefit followed, and Calvin made a surprise guest appearance. Dressed in formal white, he began to play a Chopin piece until someone plopped a summer straw hat on his head. Suddenly he thrust his head high and in a basso-falsetto burst into "In The Good Ol' Summertime." Jerry Hadley strutted out holding his straw hat aloft, and joined the singing. Seconds later the entire audience was singing and clapping as though they were at an old-fashioned hoedown.

Calvin returned home to Berkeley but for only a few days. He dined with friends, picnicked with Madi, and flew off again—this time to the Virgin Islands and his first cruise. He boarded the *Nordic Prince* in St. Thomas and joined Kent Nagano and sixty Oakland Youth Symphony Orchestra musicians for a performing tour.

The young musicians had wondered how they should talk to a *big* conductor, but Calvin made it easy by turning everything into play. He chased the teenagers up and down stairs, told jokes and shared stories about his childhood.

Although he was not a big eater, Calvin ordered doubles of favorite foods like caviar. After dinner he disco-danced. Squatting down, he put his hands behind his back and kicked up his heels. He picked up Ethel London, the orchestra's petite manager, and twirled her around. The night his name was announced as a shipboard celebrity, he let out a shriek and lay flat on the dance floor. Outside on deck, at two in the morning, he taught birdcalls to the young stay-uppers.

Much as Calvin fooled around, rehearsals were strictly business. "His hands and body told you what to do," violinist Edy Hayaska said. According to guitarist Julio Reyes, "He tactfully pushed the orchestra to its limit, giving us a burst of energy." Music was Calvin's life, but not wanting "star" treatment for doing what he loved, he allowed no one to call him *Maestro*.

The high point of the trip came when the orchestra played "The Virgin Island March" before its composer, ninety-three-year-old Alton Adams. The balding black man told the youngsters how he had conducted in shacks and concert halls during his thirty-three-year career as a navy bandmaster. His original score of the March had been lost in a fire. Although it was now the island's anthem, he had never heard the complete score.

After the Youth Symphony's first performance, Adams led them through his march once more at a faster tempo, and told them, "The world would be better off with more music."

Before they flew home, Calvin stopped to buy a three-foot-tall carved wood vase at the airport for Madi. A week later, he gave a party for the orchestra at his Berkeley home. Then he boarded a train and headed across Canada to visit his friends Richard Rodzinski and his mother Halina at Lake Placid in northern New York State. Enjoyable as the year of work had been, Calvin was exhausted. For the next several days he rarely left the Rodzinski house, except to do a little hiking and canoeing.

When Judie Janowski, his agent at Columbia Artists, Inc. (CAMI) called and asked what he was doing, he told her, "I'm sitting here in a hammock reading a book. I hope you're going to tell me the City Opera is on strike, and I don't have to come to

New York to conduct *The Magic Flute.*" He knew he also was due in Washington, D.C. to conduct a concert at the Lincoln Memorial on Labor Day before going on to New York.

On August 21, 1982, Calvin and the Rodzinskis were invited next door to a dinner party at the home of Dr. Ginger Weeks. Before the party began, Calvin set out alone for a few quiet minutes on the calm Connery Pond. On shore Laura Beattie, a vacationing teacher, admired the silhouetted canoeist and went for her camera. Moments later the weather changed and gusts of wind ruffled the water.

As Ms. Beattie came from her tent, she realized Calvin was in trouble. The wind was turning his fourteen-foot fiberglass canoe in circles. Jumping into her kayak, she paddled swiftly toward him. At the same moment, Ginger Weeks saw his trouble and swam toward the boat.

Too late! A heavy breeze capsized the canoe about fifty yards from the pond's south end. When the women reached the canoe it was empty.

Seventy state troopers, police divers and fire fighters searched for Calvin in deep, icy forty-five-degree water. One fire department diver said, "He was a smart man, but he did a dumb thing." Calvin had dressed for the night's chilly temperature in a shirt, a sweater, jeans, a corduroy jacket and tennis shoes. The clothing loaded him down—and he had disobeyed the essential boating rule. Calvin wore no life preserver!

Calvin's disappearance hit the Bay Area and the music world like a shock wave. Numbed strangers and friends wept. The teachers who had watched him grow, his colleagues who had worked with him, and his parents and intimate friends carried their pain openly. They waited, hoping the bad news would fade away. But on September 1, 1982, at 11:30 a.m. searchers found Calvin's body in murky water seventy-five yards from where the canoe had overturned.

More than two thousand fans and friends attended his funeral in San Francisco's Grace Cathedral. Had Calvin been able to comfort the crowd, many believe he would have said, "No sad hearts and no sad songs for me!"

Concertmaster Nathan Rubin and the Oakland Symphony's String Quartet opened the service. The Cathedral's Choir of boys and men sang *Amazing Grace* and the Mt. Zion Baptist District Choir sang gospel songs. Opera star Marilyn Horne sang "Softly and Tenderly" and "Nearer My God to Thee," and the TV newscaster Valerie Coleman read endless tributes from prominent people in the musical world. "He achieved so much...and has given so much to so many, that he shall not be forgotten," Kurt Adler said. Madi Bacon read the poem she composed to Calvin's last moments on earth:

..."*Gliding over the lake at dusk,*
Alone in his canoe
The bow out of the water.
Silently he paddled and drifted—
Watching the daylight fade.
Listening to the early sounds of night— . . .
He felt weightless—
A silhouette on the horizon.
Endlessly rocking between
Lake and sky
And man and music.'"

Pastor T. L. Thomas of the Mt. Zion Baptist Church where Calvin had been organist, closing the service said, "I can hear God saying, 'That's him—bring me Calvin Simmons, a man who's full of life . . . ' "

- XIX -
Calvin's Legacy

Calvin's death affected the entire Bay Area. Heavy hearted strangers and friends tried to comfort one another. Those who had enjoyed Calvin's music-making and those who wished they had seen him conduct mourned their loss.

On September 20, 1982, the Oakland Symphony gave a Memorial Concert to comfort the community, and the Paramount Theatre overflowed with grieving music lovers. Musicians and stagehands donated their services, and the contributions they collected (about $40,000) went into a Calvin Simmons Memorial Fund for young peoples' programs in the schools.

After a moment of silence, the concert opened with Madi Bacon leading the San Francisco Boys Chorus and several of its alumni through Mozart's *Ave Verum Corpus* and Ernst Bacon's *Ode to the United Nations*. Calvin had conducted both pieces as a Boys Chorus member.

Kurt Adler invited five conductors—Denis de Coteau, Edo de Waart, George Cleve, Joseph Liebling and Kent Nagano—to share the podium. Denis de Coteau, of the San Francisco Ballet, led the Los Angeles Young Musicians Foundation Debut Orchestra in the second movement, "Adagio," from Dvořák's *Symphony #8 in G*. Kent Nagano conducted Rossini's overture to *La Cenerentola* and George Cleve conducted *The Magic Flute*'s overture, which Calvin had included in his first Oakland Symphony opening-night concert. Joseph Liebling led the Memorial Concert

Chorus and John Del Carlo, through the Third Movement of Brahms's "Herr Lehre Doch Mich." Adler closed the program with a vigorous "Prelude" from Wagner's *Die Walküre*. Every number had been important to Calvin. While the music softened people's sorrow, the pain remained.

Local newspapers were filled with praise. Ernest Fleischmann called Calvin "one of the most natural musicians." Ed Korn, a friend from Calvin's opera days, said, "Underneath his impishness, he had one of the most curious minds. He had an eagerness to make things happen and he made the world come alive." Gwen Durham of San Mateo wrote, "I never met the man. I never saw him conduct but I followed his career . . . heard his music on the air. In that way our lives were shared."

Until his body was found, Beverly Sills continued to hope that he was "on the other side of the pond somewhere running around. I can't believe that that shining star is not going to flash anymore . . ." Several people composed poems with a single thought: God must have needed him to conduct His chorus of angels.

To keep Calvin's memory alive, the Oakland community named a ballroom in the Parc Oakland Hotel and a fine concert theater for him, and his figure was painted into a street mural displaying the city's many achievements.

Parents and students of the Alexander Hamilton Junior High renamed their school in his honor, and Calvin's parents presented them with a bust of Calvin sculpted by Ann Gordon-Fisher. To go with the new name students wanted a new song. So ninth grader Rhonda Riley wrote one that asked students to reach high; it closed with the phrase "We've got to try!" Their music teacher, Sharon Manuel, helped them prepare a special program at which one girl said, "We stood tall and listened with 'concert attention.'"

His life was too brief, but Calvin lived it well. He was earthy, he entertained with grace, and his spur-of-the-moment funny surprises were renown. But he was not always polite and agreeable. On rare occasions when he was displeased, his quick temper could erupt in the middle of a discussion, or he might stomp off in a snit. While it felt great to conduct a superb concert and to party afterwards, like many singles, he returned home to an empty house. There must have been times he felt lonely.

Calvin despised flattery, but bad reviews hurt. His fans watched him mature, especially in the last two years of his life when "Time" magazine called him one of America's five best up-and-coming conductors. Ernst Bacon said, "Calvin needed one more year in Vienna. Then he would have conducted Beethoven's Ninth Symphony well."

Calvin never underestimated young people. If he could have worked magic, he would have insured that every school promoted music programs. He would have given talented youngsters, especially those who could not afford instruments, the same opportunities Louise McTernan and Sidney Walker had given him. He believed that within American schools sit the future—the undiscovered composers, musicians and new audiences who need to be supported.

Calvin encouraged talent wherever he found it. When concertgoers alerted him to the young pianist Greg Tabaloff, he auditioned Greg in his own home. Mrs. Taboloff asked if this was usual, and Calvin said, "No, but I felt I should honor the audience's wishes." Then he hired Greg to play at a future concert.

Wherever Calvin went he touched someone. Julio Reyes, winner of a junior high competition, met Calvin in March 1982, when he was about to debut with the Oakland Symphony. Noticing Julio's nervousness, Calvin advised, "Do what lots of people do. Pretend everyone in the front row is naked." On the night of Julio's performance, before giving the downbeat, Calvin leaned over and imitating John Wayne's voice, he whispered, "I'll meet you at the pass."

Nikki Li Hartliep believes Calvin changed her life. In 1987 she was a winner in the Metropolitan Opera auditions. Four years earlier she had sung the lead as Cio-Cio-San in Puccini's *Madama Butterfly* in the San Francisco Opera House, and she repeated the part again in 1989. Without Calvin, Nikki Li believes she might never have become a "Merolina" or an Adler Fellow.

"I'm the oddest one to be an opera star," she said. "I'm Japanese-Italian. I was adopted by German parents when I was nine months old. There was no classical music in my family. We lived in a bush town of forty people in Alaska and I went to a one-room school house. Because I fell behind in my education, we moved to Fairbanks. I was doing poorly in bookkeeping so a high school teacher suggested I take Girls Glee Club. I thought singing would be easier. It wasn't, but I loved it. I met Calvin when he toured with WOT, and he taught a master class at the University of Alaska. (He was twenty-five years old at the time.) He told me, 'Nikki, I think you are very talented, but you have to be serious about it.'" These words sound much like the advice Max Rudolf gave Calvin at Curtis.

Nikki Li added, "I don't know what Calvin saw—something special—that I had ability, a potential. I was singing a difficult aria, and I didn't do it very well. He told me to come 'down to the States,' forgetting that Alaska was one of them. Later he sent me pamphlets from different conservatories. When I went to Chicago, I saw my first opera. I never had an opportunity to thank Calvin personally. I thank him by doing the very best I can, and I am doing the same thing he did. I am going into high schools and third and fourth grades. I tell children my story so they will know that if they want to, they can be singers too." Calvin would have liked that.

A few days before he died, Calvin asked Gerhard Samuel

(Oakland Symphony's director from 1959 to 1970) to compose and conduct a work for the 1982 celebration of the Orchestra's fiftieth season. Samuel's *The Double Concerto for Violin, Viola and Orchestra* was written during the drowning tragedy and was played during the Fall season.

Since Calvin's death, Kent Nagano's star has risen. In the past decade he has conducted The Paris Opera, in Milan's famous La Scala and in major opera houses and concert halls all over the globe. He has also recorded works with The London Symphony.

Today Kent Nagano is music director of Opera de Lyon, England's Halle Orchestra, and continues a conductor-friend relationship of almost two decades with the Berkeley Symphony Orchestra. Kent leads this small orchestra through modern music (for which they have been acclaimed) and the more traditional pieces as well.

In 1986, he was the first recipient of the $75,000 Seaver Conductor Award, receiving "the largest cash prize for an 'American conductor on the threshold of a major international career.'"

Like Calvin, Kent seeks the "inner spirit" of music. If Calvin were alive today, he would respect Kent Nagano's vast achievements.

Stories about generosity and mischief continue to pop up about Calvin. Mary Maehl recalled that after she asked whether Beethoven's "Ode to Joy" was a proper song for her daughter's wedding, he decided to play it at the ceremony. And pianist Peter Orth remembered the day Calvin decided a particular bee should not die. Patiently he chased the bee around an apartment for half an hour until he coaxed it into a jar and deposited it safely outside. Another friend laughed as he told how Calvin acted the role of maitre d' at Berkeley's popular Chez Panisse restaurant. With a towel over his arm and a joyful grin, he directed several lunchtime customers to tables. Someone said, "He shouldn't do that. It will hurt his conducting image." Calvin did not give a hoot about an image. He did not look or act like a formal conductor.

"The future changes too much," he said, so Calvin claimed he rarely made long-range plans. Nonetheless, in 1982 he was considering several projects—doing a voice-over for a film about Wagner, joining with Stevie Wonder and Herbie Mann in a jazz concert, and possibly making an appearance on his favorite soap, "General Hospital." He and Jonathan Miller had begun to talk together about doing *Don Giovanni* and the musical comedy *Kiss Me Kate*. And, he and Gordon Waldear completed a pilot for a series that would introduce different "families" of instruments. Called "Make Friends With Music," their first film featured the brass.

Today Calvin is a Bay Area legend. Every year since his death, musician-friends and community churches have given concerts in August to honor his memory.

In 1984, the California Bach Society, Edwin Flath and composer Daniel Kobialka, principal second violinist of the San Francisco Symphony, honored Calvin in Davies Hall with *Antiphony Across . . .* With Edwin Flath conducting, this premiere performance featured soprano Sheri Greenawald, a full orchestra, a large chorus, the composer as violin soloist and organist Fred Tulan.

The capacity audience heard the music begin with a bell-like hum of tuned water glasses rubbed by eighteen choristers. It suggested the sound of water lapping against a canoe. A chorus sang Kobialka's setting of five poems, including one written by Madi Bacon. The composer said he wanted people "to think of life after life . . ." and feel "it is peace." The striking evening of music reflected on Calvin's life and his work.

Calvin accomplished more in his short life than most people ever do and his legacy lives on. He lives in each of us when we sing happily in a shower or join a professional chorus. He lives on when children are introduced to music at an early age, be it at home or in school.

BETTY JANE NEVIS

Calvin and Kent Nagano, along with the young musicians
gather for a last photo after their successful tour
through the Virgin Islands.

He lives with us when corporations and individuals offer music scholarships and supply practice instruments to young people. He lives on when adults support orchestras, and his spirit lives within all of us who are keeping his ideals visible.

Those who act on Calvin's beliefs truly cause hearts to sing.

About the Author

Rinna Evelyn Wolfe is an author, educator and publisher. She holds a Master's Degree in Creative Arts and has taught all elementary school subjects including African American studies. She has also taught creative arts to teachers.

She lives in Berkeley, California and enjoys art, ballet, theater, music and outdoor sports.

Ms. Wolfe believes firmly in Calvin's philosophy, and plans to "Expand [her] mind as long as it is expandable."

About the Designer

Augustus Ginnochio is a San Francisco-based graphic artist, specializing in editorial design for performing arts organizations.

Printed by: McNaughton & Gunn in
               Saline, Michigan
               United States of America

INDEX

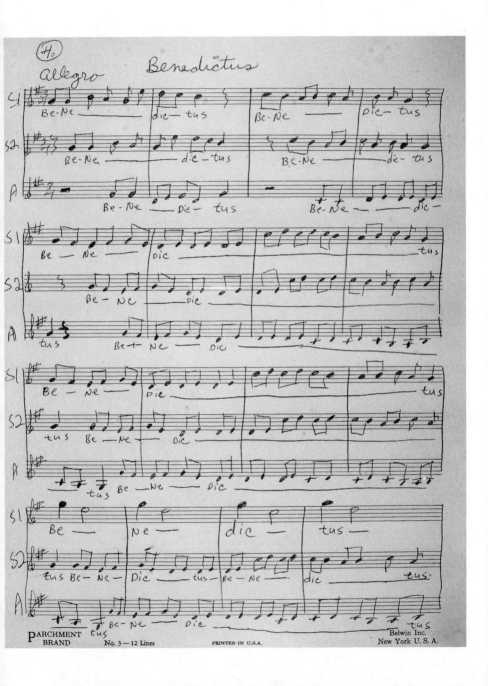